Papa's Living Room

God's Wisdom and Encouragement for Your Journey

Volume 2

By Amy Meyer

Copyright 2017. All Rights Reserved. Papa's Living Room and Thriving Culture Media.

Chief Editor: Collette Blackstone
Contributing Editor: Karen Meyer

**ISBN-13:
978-1514191002**

**ISBN-10:
1514191008**

Introduction

Hello!

I'm so glad you decided to follow that inner nudge from Papa God to pick up this book.

We all know life doesn't always make sense. There's a reason for that; God is so relational! He doesn't want us trying to figure everything out on our own. He actually wants to walk with us, converse with us, and start a dialogue with Him with the purpose of bringing about a whole new way of seeing and understanding it all. We know we can easily default and jump to conclusions on our own, but when we have our Papa God walking with us, He will widen our perspectives and bring out deeper truths of what He's really doing in us and through us. He always has a plan. He is more intentional than we realize. The evidence that this book is in your hand is proof that it's not by chance. Papa God's been orchestrating your steps to share with you what's written in these pages. He knows right where you are at, what you've been going through, and what you need to hear at this time in your life. Read it and see. Papa is ready to speak to you straight from His heart to yours.

Get ready to step out and find out how much God wants to converse with you and walk you through this journey called life. Flip to the next page to find out about the fun and creative ways this book works.

Mahalo,

Amy

HERE'S HOW IT WORKS:

The first book contains Journal Entries 1-128 of Papa God personally sharing His heart, wisdom, and encouragement with you on your journey with Him. In this second book the entries continue from 129-256.

ASK HIM WHICH JOURNAL ENTRY IS PERSONALLY FOR YOU RIGHT NOW IN YOUR LIFE. CHOOSE AN ENTRY BETWEEN NUMBERS 129-256; NEXT, FLIP THROUGH THE PAGES AND GO TO THAT ENTRY IN THIS BOOK. You can do this on your own or in a group setting. You'll be amazed at how accurate and straight to the heart they are! God knows what you need before you ask Him, and He knows what's written on these pages. He always wants to speak to you, and He will reveal to you the number that's just for you right now.

HERE ARE A COUPLE WAYS YOU'LL HEAR HIM: He'll either show you the number in your mind as you ask Him for it, or He'll whisper it to your heart. You really do hear Him and He hears you. He's going to show you just how much through these pages.

My sheep listen to my voice, and I know them, and they follow me.

John 10:27

Table of Contents

Entries 129-257

Experiencing the Atmosphere of Heaven on Earth............pg. 1
Entry #129
You Are Growing New Muscles of Surrender......................pg. 3
Entry #130
What Must I Do?.............pg. 6
Entry #131
What You Were Created For....pg. 8
Entry #132
Resting on the Cornerstone.....pg. 10
Entry #133
Time Is an Investment......pg. 12
Entry #134
It's Going To Be Worth It......pg. 14
Entry #135
Let Go of the Old, Embrace the New..................................pg. 15
Entry #136
Grounds for Leadership.....pg. 17
Entry #137

I Am Transforming You....pg. 18
Entry #138
Declare, Pick Up Your Sword, and Stand..................pg. 20
Entry #139
Your Release Is Drawing Near...pg. 22
Entry #140
Faith Is Substance...Who Are You Giving It To?............pg. 24
Entry #141
Why You Were Created......pg. 26
Entry #142
What Does "Tending To" Mean to You..............................pg. 28
Entry #143
My Love Is Potent Enough to Persuade You.........................pg. 30
Entry #144
Give Your Mind a Rest........pg. 32
Entry #145
Your Life Is Like a Book........pg. 34
Entry #146
All I Want Is You..................pg. 37
Entry #147
Bask in My Goodness......................pg. 39
Entry #148
I Long To Be Loved by You..................................pg. 41
Entry #149

I Am Pleased with Your Change of Heart..................pg. 43
Entry #150

I Am Everything You're Looking For..................pg. 45
Entry #151

Your Training Will Pay Off..................pg. 47
Entry #152

I Will Make Up the Time..................pg. 50
Entry #153

This Is Your True REALITY..................pg. 52
Entry #154

Your Goliaths Are Coming Down..................pg. 54
Entry #155

Under Persecution..................pg. 55
Entry #156

Making It through the Rough Terrain..................pg. 57
Entry #157

Trust the Process..................pg. 59
Entry #158

The Peace That Surpasses..................pg. 62
Entry #159

The Plow..................pg. 64
Entry #160
The Reinforcement of Worship..................pg. 67
Entry #161
What You Look Like to Your Enemies..................pg. 69
Entry #162
You're Advancing in Your Training..................pg. 71
Entry #163
Release Your Family to Me..................pg. 73
Entry #164
Learning How to Receive..................pg. 75
Entry #165
You Are Complete in Me..................pg. 78
Entry #166
Fitted with Honor.......pg. 80
Entry #167
Delays Are Not Denials..................pg. 82
Entry #168
Delays Are Laced with Purpose and Possibilities..................pg. 84
Entry #169

Focus on Today..........pg. 86
Entry #170
Walking into Your Future......................pg. 87
Entry #171
I Burn with Desire for You........................pg. 89
Entry #172
You Are a Gateway Anchored in Me..........................pg. 92
Entry #173
Hidden from the Enemy's Radar......................pg. 94
Entry #174
You Are My Scribe........pg. 96
Entry #175
Starting Your Day Out Right........................pg. 98
Entry #176
Gift of Healing..............pg. 100
Entry #177
Bulletproof Mindset.........pg. 102
Entry #178
Focused and Equipped........................pg. 104
Entry #179
Simply Ask Me................pg. 106
Entry #180

The Foundation Is Finished; It's Time to Build..........pg. 108
Entry #181
Be Encouraged...............pg. 110
Entry #182
I Am the One Renewing You................pg. 112
Entry #183
How to Reap a Massive Harvest...............pg. 114
Entry #184
It's Time for the Curtain to Be Drawn..............pg. 116
Entry #185
A Perfect Place to Be.............pg. 118
Entry #186
It's Time to Align.........pg. 120
Entry #187
It's Time to Put On the Shoes.................pg. 121
Entry #188
I'm Proud of You..........pg. 123
Entry #189
Your Friend the Gardener.................pg. 125
Entry #190

Reaching Beyond the Vine..........................pg. 127
Entry #191
The Gift of the Heart........................pg. 129
Entry #192
Engage the Creation Center I've Given You......................pg. 132
Entry #193
Confounded by Laughter....................pg. 135
Entry #194
My Way to Prosperity......pg. 136
Entry #195
Some Questions to Consider When Managing a Company..........................pg. 138
Entry #196
It's Not That Complicated....................pg. 140
Entry #197
You Are My Delight..........................pg. 142
Entry #198
A Simple Act of Faith..........................pg. 144
Entry #199
You're Going to Like the End Result........................pg. 147
Entry #200

The Proving of Your Faith through Testing..................pg. 150
Entry #201
The Treasure of UNDERstanding......................pg. 152
Entry #202
Rest Your Soul in Me..................................pg. 154
Entry #203
Faith of a Child................pg. 156
Entry #204
The Boomerang Effect: Accusations..................pg. 158
Entry #205
Friends of the Gardener......................pg. 160
Entry #206
Answered Prayers and Switching Kingdoms....................pg. 163
Entry #207
I'm Giving the Baton to You, Now Run!............................pg. 166
Entry #208
This Storm Will Pass............................pg. 168
Entry #209
About Emotions............pg. 170
Entry #210

Advancement Is a Choice..................pg. 172
Entry #211
An Introduction to Your Music Class...................pg. 174
Entry #212
Limitless Freedom.......pg. 177
Entry #213
The Puzzle Piece Called Choice...................pg. 179
Entry #214
Understanding the Power of Your Will...................pg. 181
Entry #215
Patient Pursuit..............pg. 183
Entry #216
Are You Ready for the Ride of a Lifetime?...................pg. 185
Entry #217
Prepare for Take-off: 10...9...8...7...6..............pg. 187
Entry #218
Calculated Risks............pg. 189
Entry #219
You're My Voice in the Earth...................pg. 191
Entry #220
Adapting to the Passenger Seat...................pg. 194
Entry #221

Your Victory Is Just a Belief Away..................pg. 196
Entry #222
Investment and Harvest....................pg. 198
Entry #223
Come In and Dine with Me.......................pg. 200
Entry #224
Slam the Door on the Enemy's Fingers......................pg. 203
Entry #225
My Promise and Commitment to You.............................pg. 206
Entry #226
The Awakening Has Begun......................pg. 208
Entry #227
Stay Diligent and Trust Me....pg. 210
Entry #228
Illusions......................pg. 212
Entry #229
Faith to Step Out............................pg. 214
Entry #230
Today..................pg. 217
Entry #231
The Marking of Peace.............................pg. 219
Entry #232

In Between the Sets of Waves..................pg. 221
Entry #233
Combating Fear and Frustration..................pg. 224
Entry #234
A Good Dose of Meditation..................pg. 227
Entry #235
The Beauty Aid..................pg. 229
Entry #236
Take Flight for New Sight..................pg. 232
Entry #237
You Will Make It!..................pg. 235
Entry #238
Safe Guard Your Decisions..................pg. 237
Entry #239
Your Heavenly Language and Spiritual Growth..................pg. 239
Entry #240
Depression..................pg. 242
Entry #241
Enjoying the Fruit of Your Labor..................pg. 245
Entry #242

My Delight Is a Light for All to See..................pg. 247
Entry #243
The Invitation to Enroll Further in My Training.....................pg. 249
Entry #244
How to Have More of an Effortless Life and Healthy Friendships.....pg. 252
Entry #245
We Want to be With You All the Time..........................pg. 255
Entry #246
Are You Guessing at How to Live Your Life?..........................pg. 257
Entry #247
One of Your Greatest Weapons of Defense....................pg. 260
Entry #248
Rest: The Ultimate Trademark................pg. 262
Entry #249
I Will Take You Through the Storm........................pg. 264
Entry #250
Surrender in Action........................pg. 266
Entry #251
The I.D. Check on Provision....................pg. 269
Entry #252

No Need to Apologize........pg. 272
Entry #253
Why Is Stillness a Challenge?.........................pg. 275
Entry #254
What's My Responsibility?....................pg. 278
Entry #255
Recommendations from Your Heart Doctor................................pg. 280
Entry #256
How Does Faith Come?...............................pg. 283
Entry #257

Papa's Living Room Vol. 2

Experiencing the Atmosphere of Heaven on Earth

Entry #129

Come to Me out of your free will. It should never be forced. I love you more than you know. I want you to pay attention to the atmosphere of My Kingdom. My desire is for it to be seen and experienced in the earth as it is in heaven. You are My carrier of it. Tell Me, Sweet One, what do My Scriptures say heaven is like? What do the stories you've heard say it is like?

I desire you to live in a state of heaven on earth. I know it is a foreign concept to many, but heaven and I are more real than the air you breathe. Did I not tell you that the kingdom of God is within you? What do you think that looks like, sounds like, smells like, and feels like? I am in you, the hope of glory!

Come on, take a guess, tell me what My kingdom is like, and I will confirm it to you. Look around you and see My kingdom in the earth. Taste My kingdom in the earth. Smell My kingdom in the earth. Hear My kingdom in the earth. Anything that is good, precious, and pure, is of Me. Look for me, like hidden treasure, for I have hidden Myself throughout creation hoping to be discovered by you. I am fascinating and My desire is to fascinate you.

I have placed many things in the earth for you to enjoy. My love provides the greatest gifts; creation is one of them. So, look for yourself…listen, touch, hear, smell, and see all My goodness poured out for you!

You Are Growing New Muscles of Surrender

Entry #130

You are growing new muscles of surrender. Don't be so hard on yourself if you don't get this down the first time. I am training you just like a fitness coach trains his client. Yes, I know you're a little sore, but that's OK because I have great news! New muscles of submission are being built in you that will give you the staying power to remain with Me and not to venture out in the opposite strength of your flesh. This takes work, of course. Your flesh can be a bit demanding. You must allow Me to become greater than it, in your mind.

I often find you thinking of ways to rule your life if My way doesn't work. You come up with your Plan A; and Plan B, if Plan A doesn't work. Can you really trust yourself? Where is that getting you?

Think about it... if I'm a God that cannot lie and I know everything, why wouldn't My plan work? Could it be that you struggle to trust Me because I do things in a way you wouldn't think or naturally choose? I do that on purpose you know. I'm allowing it to cause you to give up your limited human ideas and wisdom and simply trust Me. Life is a lot easier that way, don't you think?

Why are you trying to figure so many things out? Do you think that I can't see your needs or desires? Why are you looking to yourself for the solutions? Isn't that a bit heavy to carry? Your fleshly nature longs to appease itself with a sense of being in control. But since you enlisted into My training course, I am building your spirit man up. In your flesh, you want an instant fix, but I am teaching you longevity and stamina. That is why some things are not happening as quickly as you'd like. Endurance is another thing I am adding to you.

I am focused on the inside of you. I am building in you a vessel that will truly be able to contain all that I have in store for you! That is why this "class" is taking longer. Look at it in construction terms. The bigger the house plan the longer it takes to craft and build. It is carrying a greater purpose. It could be that you've been thinking too small, thinking in ways of how you could obtain with your own strength and skill. Let Me reassure you...I am thinking far greater than that! I know what I have created you for. You may not see it yet. Know that I am an excellent trainer and developer. Lean into Me, yield to My processes, and allow Me to draw out your full potential.

What Must I Do?

Entry #131

You have asked me the question, "Lord, what must I do?" "Do?" I question. "Haven't I already done everything?"

What more could you do? If you are trying to "do," it means you are trying to "earn." What could you possibly earn from Me that I haven't already given you? I don't want you to be focused on self-works. It can become a great trap that ensnares many of My children. Refuse to go down the path of self-works. Only walk the path of My grace. The reason it becomes a snare to you is that it's anchored in your ego. The ego wants to be appreciated for the work it's done. It longs for accolades and strokes for its own ability. When you operate from this place, it's as though you are trying to earn my appreciation or gain credit from Me. This is how the world operates, but it is not how I operate. Love has no expectations or measuring chart for value. I know you're longing to be needed and valued, but you already are! You are created for My affection. I long to shower you with My affection. But how can I, if your receiver is turned off?

Oh, Sweet One, how silly it is to think you could do anything for Me. I created you to be loved by Me and to do things together like best friends. I didn't create you to do things for Me like servants do. I have a whole host of heavenly beings and angels that assist and wait on Me. No, you are My sons and daughters, not servants. Am I an impersonal God? Wouldn't you be making me out to be quite impersonal if all I wanted and created you for was just to serve Me? No, that is what religion has taught you, but that is not who I am. I am your true, original Father and My heart aches for you like any good Father's would! Why do you think you have the mutual hunger in you that aches for Me? Your free and fun life can be with Me!

What You Were Created For

Entry #132

Always remember that you were created for love. This teaching about service/obligation has nothing to do with Me! It is an old lie of the enemy that he has used for centuries! He uses it to keep My people committed to works instead of to love. Works always keep you at a distance, because no matter how much you do, you could always do more... leaving you feeling like a failure; never good enough to "make Me happy." Am I a fickle God that way? What this does is create in you a completely wrong mindset that holds you hostage and distorts My loving nature.

Do you think Jesus came to this earth with only a checklist and a mindset of service and works to accomplish... or was it a demonstration and sacrifice of his love for Me? He chose to do this out of His own free will. Love compelled Him, not a checklist. It was truly out of love. Do you realize that even in your own efforts you can't love Me enough? Only through and by living in the sacrifice of My son can you be satisfied. It is by grace. His gift was more than enough! I am completely satisfied.

So what about you? You were made to be loved, now live loved. Let Me handle all the rest. Live a life full of rejoicing! Since the battle has been won and all is complete, now live a life of victory!!

Resting on the Cornerstone

Entry #133

Can you see what I am doing in you? Oh, what a beautiful work it is! I am setting you in as a living stone, perfectly fit in Me. I (Christ) am the Cornerstone. Papa has been carefully carving you to fit in Me with no gaps showing. He has been carving you to the point where you and I look like one solid rock together! Oh, how beautiful it is! Yes, now you will be able to hold the weightier things of My Kingdom for you are no longer resting upon yourself, but upon Me. As you remain at rest upon and in Me, you will be unmovable and unshaken. I have made you to perfectly fit Me.

I have many things in store for you this next season. Many things you have long awaited for! Yes, they are starting to take root now! A great season awaits you! So be not disheartened, but truly believe, for you have chosen to be seated in Me. You shall fulfill through Me all that I have asked of you. Oh, yes! What glorious days await you!

Time Is an Investment

Entry #134

Time is an investment so invest in what matters most right now. Time-eaters eat away at your strength. Strength is stored for accomplishing a task. What are the tasks that I've asked you to put your hand to? Strength is in the hand is it not?
Be careful what you reach for. Ask yourself, "Is this where God wants me to apply my time and strength?"

Watch out for the little foxes of reason, doubt, distraction and logic.
They gnaw away at your new upstarts. Now is the time to be single minded and invest in what I've called you to. Can waste produce anything? I think you know the answer to that. So, stay far away from the time-wasters. Only give your time and seed to that which I have

called you to. Even if by appearance it looks like a good thing, test all things by simply asking the Holy Spirit, who lives inside of you, if it's for you. There are such things as illusions and mirages. That is why you must not judge by appearance; only by the Spirit.

Test all things and follow My lead. You will avoid much trouble and heartache. Invest your time in Me. This is one investment you'll always, always profit from! Those who seek Me will find Me. Those who invest in what I've given them to do will reach the heights of their full potential! Be a good farmer. Protect what I've given you. Be aware of your time frame and be diligent to plant.

It's Going to Be Worth It

Entry #135

Keep your eyes on Me. Look not on the natural. Remember, My Spirit always prepares things in the unseen first. Live in and through the unseen. That is where I want you to reside. Continue to make your residence in Me. You are My child. I am taking care of you. Oh, if you only knew the things I have deposited in you... You shall see their fruit one day soon and you shall agree with Me that everything you have gone through will have all been worth it!!

Let Go of the Old, Embrace the New

Entry #136

I have been untangling you from the snares and the entrapments of the flesh these last seasons. At times, you have experienced the pain of this, because I have been chiseling away a false identity you have. Yes, you have felt lost in this process at times, but in reality, the opposite is happening. You are discovering your true self in Me. I am lightening the load and making it easier for you to grasp. It's OK for you to let go of the old and embrace the new!

For anything to be restored, it must first be stripped down. Trust Me, that I am a good Father and I know what I am doing. Lean into Me and not to your own understanding. Rest and allow the process to happen.

Grounds for Leadership

Entry #137

I have been preparing spiritual ground inside of you. In this ground, I will plant My ways of leadership, and you will produce and implement it in the true way. You will be able to detect the false, immediately. I am granting to you the eyes to see in the Spirit.

This is coming to you in greater dimension this year. Keep your heart soft and pliable. Train your mind to be solely fixed on Me. Holy Spirit will help you in this. My purpose for you has been established long before you entered the earth. I will have my way with you. Enter all the things that I have been showing you, such as the way My kingdom operates.

I Am Transforming You

Entry #138

There are so many things I want to do in you. Keep submitting your life to Me. Do you know who you're submitting to? The One who is the keeper of everything! You are in the hands of your Maker who wants the best for you. Just keep letting Me have My way.

I am transforming you to where many will see the most beautiful, interesting aspect of Me in you. Many of these things are hidden in you right now, but they are developing and surely will manifest on the outside of you when the time is right, just like the development of a butterfly. The butterfly was inside the cocoon all along, was it not? Wait till you see what I've placed inside of you!!

Always think bigger! The enemy would like to keep you thinking small so that you will only manifest a small amount. Thinking big is the button that releases faith! Anything seems impossible until someone does it! Faith unrolls your butterfly wings. It takes faith to stretch them out. But once you feel the wind of My spirit fill them, it's easy to take the leap! Give Me your wings to fill and I'll do the rest!

Declare, Pick Up Your Sword and Stand

Entry #139

You are called to lead the way. Declare who my people are, and point them to their Source--Me. I will cause you to rip the scales from their eyes and expose every lie they've believed. Through Me you will restore to them their victory and rightful place in Me.

You will hand back to My people the swords they've dropped years ago. These are swords of authority, swords of eternal victory. These swords were meant to defeat the enemy always! The sword of the Holy Spirit shall return to them in great power! They shall be transformed as you hand these back to them.

Call My people to stand up and fight the good fight of faith again! Weariness has robbed them far too long. I say, "No more!" Today is a new day. Take your swords and stand My people! Move in My strength for today is the day of victory!

Your Release Is Drawing Near

Entry #140

The timing of your release is drawing near. Finish sweeping out everything that's not of Me. I need you alert and ready; for when I blow My trumpet, I need you to act! See in the Spirit, for the spirit realm is truly so much more powerful and real than the natural one you live in. It's time to live fully in your spirit man. You can groom your spirit man by praying much in the gift of tongues by the Holy Spirit. Adore this position and live in it and you will thrive.

I have adorned you with many riches. Soon you will see them manifested in the earth. I trust you with them and know that you will heed my every command with these resources. Truly you will be blessed! Every need will be met in your household. You will be one who will lend and not borrow. I will prosper you and you will enjoy the rich pleasures of My goodness.

Just as a grape is crushed and contained until the appointed day of its release, so have you gone through this process of allowing Me to have My way and work maturity in you. There is a high price put on your name! For you have allowed Me to crush you, contain you, and re-form you. Oh! What an amazing flavor and aroma you are going to have! It will be like none other! Truly authentic! That is why there will be a high price placed on your name. You will taste like Me!

Thank you for enduring the process. Your time of release is coming. It's coming!

Faith Is Substance...Who Are You Giving It To?

Entry #141

Faith is what gives Me power and access to act in your life, or gives the enemy power and access to act. You only have two places to place your faith: either in what I'm saying or in what the enemy is saying. I have spoken much on the earth about the importance of believing Me. Faith, from heaven's standpoint, is considered more valuable than the highest priced gems and gold. Faith is the only substance that either I or the enemy can stand on. Why else would the enemy be after your mind and ability to create with your words. What you act upon or act out upon stems from what you believe in your mind and heart.

If you'll allow Me to fill you by spending time with Me, I will transform you by renewing your mind. This comes through knowing My love for you and experiencing My presence. The attacks the enemy throws at you will lessen, since he will have no substance to stand on. For you have turned from his lies and given your faith to Me, a gift of beautiful, priceless faith.

Why You Were Created

Entry #142

What did I pay for when My Son died on the Cross? Did I pay to hire a bunch of workers? If I am all-knowing and all powerful, do I really need workers? Have I not created all the heavenly hosts to assist Me? Can the very man I Myself created, help Me?

Let's go back to the beginning. What was man created for? Was it not recorded in My book of Genesis, "Let us make man in our own likeness, image, and behavior..."?

And is not My nature the purest form of love? Why do you think We created man? Since We are love, then how can We express that love when there is no one to love and walk together with? You were created for love.

Let's fast forward to the Cross. Do you remember what Jesus said His desire was? *"Father, I pray that they will all be one, just as you and I are one--as you are in me, Father, and I am in you. And may they be in us so that the world will believe you sent me." (John 17:21)* Or, did He say, *"Father, here are your workers..."* Did I bring you back with My Son's painful death, just so you could work for Me? May I ask, "Where is the love in that?" Is that what My Son died for? Would anyone die for a "cause" like that? Or was there a desire far beyond your human reasoning and explanations? Have you ever noticed that love does the unreasonable, my child? Was it reasonable for Christ to die on the cross for you? What do you think caused Him to do that out of His own free will? There is only one answer My dear one, the unreasonable act of LOVE! You were created for Love!

"Embracing what God does for you, is the best thing you can do for Him." Romans 12:2 Msg.

What Does "Tending To" Mean to You

Entry #143

If Adam was created for work, wouldn't he have had to plan the garden, till it, and plant it? Tell Me... Doesn't My Word say that I, Elohim, planted the garden and set Adam in it? It says also that Adam tended to the garden. What if "tended to" actually meant to adore and love back. What if "tended to" simply demonstrated a joyful, loving experience in taking care of what I had already given him as we shared it together? What if "tending to" is simply adoring, enjoying, partaking, creating, and sharing. Are these not generously shared within a healthy relationship?

Nothing Adam ever did was done alone. I

was always with Him through My creation, walking with him in the cool of the day, naming animals together, and simply resting with him in spirit. Man, is never alone.

I am the All Seeing One and the All Knowing One. Seek Me for the answers you are looking for. Instead of looking at our relationship like work, consider the definition I just gave you and let's "tend to" each other together. Don't you think that's much more enjoyable...?

My Love Is Potent Enough to Persuade You

Entry #144

What did My son pay for to bring back to Me? Was it not you and all of mankind? Why? What was I after? Let's just say, if you had lost the love of your life in war and determined to get him or her back, wouldn't you do anything to find him or her and bring him or her home safely? Wouldn't you want to restore him or her and re-engage in the love and passion you share together? There is nothing like the power of love! Nothing can compare to it. My love has chased after you and found you! And I won't let go! I've paid too high of a price to lose you! Yes, you've always had the freedom to walk away, just as any lover does; but I believe in My love for you, that it's more powerful and potent enough to persuade you from any other substitute. We were designed for each other! Those who put their love and trust in Me shall never be disappointed. Trust in My wisdom and lean into My love. I'm the One you've been searching for, and I have sought and found you.

Give Your Mind a Rest

Entry # 145

You can't find all the answers within yourself, even with your self-analysis. Stop trying to figure everything out! It's a self-protection mechanism. This can border on the behavior of an orphan, you know. Are you an orphan? Of course, not! You have the best thing you could ever have, and that's Me!

I really am real, you know that? Just because you can't feel me all the time doesn't mean I'm not there. Can you feel the people around you when you walk through a store? But aren't they there? Trust Me, I always have My eyes upon you.

If you want to experience Me, you're going

to have to believe in Me from your heart, not your mind. Your mind will dismantle your belief like construction workers dismantle a building. Faith is not found in the mind, faith is found in the heart, just like love. It's how I've designed you. So, give your mind a rest and sit back and trust. Not with your mind, remember, but with a childlike heart. There you go!

Your Life Is Like a Book

Entry# 146

Books are used to tell stories; life stories, for example. The divisions that divide a book are called chapters, right? When you read the chapters, they take you through a journey. What would a book be without its chapters and the chapters without their details? What would happen if you rushed through a book or skipped through the chapters? You wouldn't get the whole story and you'd miss some important keys. Life is your journey, and I have written about your life page by page. Prophesies are like the table of contents or the title page in a book, that lets you know what's up ahead. I know your end from your beginning. My plans for you are good to give you a future and a hope!

Books are also used to educate with outlined information and principles to apply in your life. I have given you personal insight through your personal prophecies and through My Word as to how to align with your destiny. I've already laid out the outcome. How wonderful it is! But what would happen if someone read a book but forgot or didn't apply what it said? Do you think they would have the same outcome their book purposed?

This is a team effort. You can't go out with a plan to plant tomatoes, never plant the seeds, and then get angry at Me because the tomatoes never showed up. I've given you everything you need to prosper in this life, and my grace is there to assist you all the way. The seeds are already within you. Draw them up and begin to plant, and you will surely have the outcome promised to you in the book of your life.

I am for you, not against you! All My promises are "Yes" and "Amen" for those who step out in faith. Only believe and act upon that belief. All things are possible to those who believe. Set your sights, read your prophesies, and plan accordingly. I've already forecasted how I want your book to end. Join me in the journey and let's enjoy this fine book of yours!

All I Want Is You

Entry #147

Now you're getting it! All I want is you! Let Me do all the work. I have paved the way so that we could just enjoy each other and walk together. Look at Enoch. Didn't the Bible say that he was a man that walked with God? Yes! He was and is such a delight to Me!

I am not into the works of man. All it does is pull them away from Me. It is not a weak thing to depend on Me and follow My ways, you know. It is truly the essence of a lover leaning on her beloved. Nothing is stronger than love, for love is of Me. It comes straight from Me. Love is light! It expels all darkness. Why did I say in My word to make love your highest pursuit? When you share love, live in love, and live loved your reason for existence is accomplished. All your needs are eternally met. Fear is cast out for eternity and you are forever kept in safety. Nothing can break My bond of love!

Let love be your highest pursuit! When you are pursuing Me, this is what you're doing. Oh, how I will fill you up! I will fill you so full you won't be able to contain it, and it will constantly be spilling out onto others! Once they taste My love, they will always come back for more. Nothing on earth tastes better than My love!

Bask in My Goodness

Entry #148

So, you may ask, how do I get love? My answer to you is to simply "be." Open your arms and receive the bounty! It's not for sale; you can't earn it. It is freely given out of the goodness of My heart. It is My joy to give it to you. Choose to be a part of who I am. Continue to step into Me and out of yourself. Bask in My goodness like in a fine bath drawn full of My flowers, full of My fragrance, full of My oils, full of My delightful essence.

Bask in Me, for today and from here on out I am giving you "dove's eyes"; eyes for Me alone. There is a great purity coming to you. I am restoring your heart. I see you stepping out of the old and into a place of purity that hasn't been reached up to this point. Yes, I am giving you doves' eyes and a heart of gold.

You are so precious to Me and My desire is to care for you like a dove. From here on out you will carry My love, gentleness, and purity wherever you go. Today I am wiping you clean. You will feel and even begin to smell the freshness of your soul. Child-likeness is returning to you. New days are arising. I see the sunlight brushing across your feathers and reflecting in your eyes. It is the light of My salvation that is right before you. Stay nurtured in My hands, for this is the place where you will find rest and be fed. I am gentle with you and I am caring for you. Keep your eyes on Me.

I Long to Be Loved by You

Entry #149

What happens when people are in love? All they can do is see and think about that person. All their circumstances and situations fade in comparison to the one they love, the one that's always on their mind. Their love consumes them and those around them.

Let Me consume you with My fullness, where all you can see is My continued goodness. I long to be the focus of your attention. Do you know what that will do for you? How do you think your life will change? Do you think you'll worry as much? My church is often looking everywhere else but to Me. They're looking to programs, quick fixes, substitutes, and mostly to their self-will. Being in love is a lot easier and more enjoyable!

How does one fall in love again? Love can come forth by way of adoring, admiring, appreciating, and being attracted to. When was the last time you stopped, and thought about Me in these ways? Let's go away to a quiet place like lovers do. You pick the place and surprise Me with your favorite spot, and there let's enjoy admiring each other. Are you afraid of My love? Is that why you are afraid to come? Are you afraid of your inadequacies? Close your eyes and imagine Me handing you a ticket that says "Inadequacies cleared: Paid in Full"! Now open your eyes! It's for real! I've paid for them. Please, take the ticket from Me. Accept it. It makes Me smile when you do. Now, let's go and enjoy adoring one another.

I Am Pleased with Your Change of Heart

Entry #150

I am pleased with your change of heart, the change of truly surrendering all your self-efforts to Me to bring about your dreams and calling. This is not in vain. You shall truly begin to see My hand at work, now that you have removed yours.

Your journey is about ready to get a whole lot better. Continue to fill yourself with My Word. It is like oil, smooth to your spiritual joints, or like primer as I layer color upon you. Spend much time in the gospels and especially in the epistles. Read a portion of both when you read. I am building a house in you that shall stand till the very end. Oh, what a fine work I'm doing in and through you!

Yes, one day you'll step back and see that masterpiece I've created. Nobody else is like you! You're My one and only. I understand you and your ins and outs. I made you and am satisfied with the progression of things. Keep saying yes to me and keep yielding your structure to My hands. You are a fine piece in the making, and I love you dearly.

I Am Everything You're Looking For

Entry #151

I have planted you into My Son like the grapevine and its branches, in John 15. I have planted you there so that you may bear fruit in abundance! My Son is pure and good. Would you really want to be anywhere else?

My Son is the Vine and you are the branches. You bring Me such great joy when you display the fruits of love, joy, peace, patience, kindness, goodness, faithfulness, gentleness, and self-control. You bring others great joy as well. Apart from My Son, these are much harder to obtain. You can try with all your might, but you will only yield a very small amount. So, what about all your labor?

Is it really worth it for pride's sake? Isn't it easier just to connect to Him and glean from His supplies? They are freely given, you know...

Can you really fuel yourself? Is your make-up to be fully self-contained, or is that the mindset of the world? Who made you? Do you think the Designer might know the truth about the make, model and function of the design He made? Hmm... So, can you fuel yourself, or do you find yourself often feeling hungry with an inner pain unsatisfied no matter what or who you try to hook up to? Out of many keys, isn't there usually only one key that fits the lock? You are the lock and I am the Key, the only one that's designed to fit the hole in your heart. Give up on all the other "keys" and try the key that fits. You'll be amazed at the life that will come flowing into you!! I have and am everything you're looking for!

Your Training Will Pay Off

Entry #152

Do not be discouraged because "the call" didn't come in the way you thought it would or in the time frame you expected. Some are called to be decorative lawn trees and others are called to be mighty oak trees. Your training has been longer, because I have called you to no small thing. You must be able to handle the weight of it. I've been taking you through a spiritual version of kingdom Green Beret training. I know it's been hard, and not everyone can make it through this, but I also know what I've made you for and the potential I've placed inside of you. I understand your pain as you watch others graduate from smaller ranks, receiving their emblems of authority; entering their missions. I've seen your heart sink and have heard your cry, as you continue forward still in your training. Oh, but know this, it will pay off!! You are of a special kind of ranking, built for special assignments.

No longer compare yourself with the others. Keep your heart right and honor Me. Know your service is judged only by Me. I am not comparing you to anyone else. I only want you to keep your heart right and surrendered, trusting My wisdom as I lead you down a path not many travel. It is only for the brave of heart. Trust that I know what you can handle and won't lead you astray. Trust in the abilities I've placed within you and continue to follow My lead. A true soldier only obeys the orders of his leader.
You are doing well. Turn your ear away from the naysayers. They do not know you nor the path you are traveling on. I'm making you bulletproof to the enemy's attacks! I'm raising your spiritual endurance levels. I'm adding strength and wisdom to you. You can't see this all right now, but you will. Yield and trust; don't

try to use your brain. Just yield and trust, putting one step in front of the other. Many are called, but few are chosen and I have chosen you, great soldier!

I Will Make Up the Time

Entry #153

Didn't you commit your life to Me? Then know that I will bring about every promise I've given you. You're closer than you think to see many things come to pass. I will make up the time that you feel has been lost. I have been adding great wisdom to you. Do not look at your age. Look at the fine, valuable wine I am producing in you.

Stop believing that the call hasn't happened because of something you haven't done. Am I truly that limited by you? I know your heart and that it is willing to follow Me. There's no need for any regret. What do you truly regret? I will use every single piece of the journey to elevate you. You will be glad that you went through it all! You will see My hand of provision. Just do your best to follow and yield. You can have a cheerful heart if you focus on the right things. If you do, your emotions will change. Change your focus.

I will always provide you with the best! You are Mine. Keep your thoughts on Me and off yourself. I am the strong one you can lean on. Your frustrations will turn into delight. You don't have to know everything, just know that you're in Me and you're not going to miss it! Let your heart be so full of worship that there's no room for worry! That will elevate you on a much higher playing field, even above your enemies!!

This Is Your True REALITY

Entry #154

I am doing such a work in you. I am clearing away all the debris of unbelief! You are rising into whom I say you are! You are rising! The barriers that once stopped you are now being removed. I am bringing prosperity to you. It's on its way! Keep expecting My goodness. Keep expecting the answers to your prayers! Only believe, only believe! All things are possible. Only believe!

Stand in who you are in Me. That is the REALITY! Stand in your place of authority! Go over your prophetic words! Pick up your sword and use it! Decree and declare and it will be established! Just as a king or queen's words establish, so I have called you and appointed you with authority as My daughter to rule and establish the territories I've given you. Rule with Me! People are waiting for you to decree to set them free, to make straight the path! You have what you need now. Go! Make My name great for the land rejoices when My people rule.

Your Goliaths Are Coming Down

Entry #155

Use the voice I have given you. Speak My words; declare with a mighty sound! Play boldly the instruments I've given you. The goliaths that once came against you and caused you to run are coming down; and they are coming down with great force, because I am with you!
You've changed your mindset and are refusing the lies, for you have taken up your stance in Me! I am rejoicing as I stand with you for I have already given you the victory! Shout your praise and strike terror in your enemy for we have overcome! Now walk and talk like it! The authority is yours. I've given it to you!

Under Persecution

Entry #156

You are more precious to Me than you know! I have seen the struggle you've been going through. Continue to patiently endure and I will cause things to begin to change to your advantage. Don't allow the comments to bother you and affect you so badly. Just know that if you're standing up for Me and My truth, you will face persecution.

Therefore, rejoice, for it shows that you are on the right track. It shows you are Mine, because you would rather believe Me and follow My ways than man's traditions. I am pleased and very blessed! You are passing your tests.

Know that in the days ahead you will meet My people, those who are of like heart, your true brothers and sisters. You have been faithful and I will reward you.

I know that you aren't trying to earn anything from Me. But because I love you, I want to give you the desires of your heart. Rest in Me. Keep close to Me. I am your Father and a good shepherd. Draw everything you need from Me.

Making It through the Rough Terrain

Entry #157

Everything is going to be alright. I am ordering your steps. Don't worry, I have a plan and will unveil it soon. Please, Sweet One, try not to question Me so much. Just flow with Me and turn aside from your own understanding. If I have promised in My Word that I order your steps, then believe that I am doing so. I am a God that cannot lie.

I am fully aware of your needs. I know you have financial needs. Know that I see it all and will not allow you to stumble. You are going to make it!

Keep climbing by faith, even though it seems painful at times. I have my eyes on you. Don't lose heart. Keep yourself grounded and at rest in Me, not in the troubled terrain. Keep your eyes of faith on Me. Remember my son, Peter? If you keep your eyes on Me, putting one step in front of the other, you'll overcome the impossible! Eyes off self and onto Me. Find the good in your present circumstances and you'll ignite a heart of worship to lead you like a light, right on through.

Trust the Process

Entry #158

There are many days of release in life, not just one "Day of Release." Religion has made it bigger than it is. Releases come in levels. If you miss the importance of each level, you'll fail to see them as important building stones. Many times, we want to rush past or through them, because we fail to understand what they are about at the time. Our eyes are often only set on one goal--our "ultimate arrival" in life. Yes, there are times of great victory, but they should never negate the trying times as something to be avoided. In fact, it was those times of difficulty that produced great character and stamina in you.

Life is a progression of releases -- each

one necessary, each one important. Look at Joseph's life: The night dreams that were released to him. The day the beautiful coat was released to him. The day his brothers released him into the well. The day his brothers released him to the slave traders. The day Potiphar released him from the slave traders. The day Potiphar released him over his household. The day Potiphar's wife released his garments. The day Potiphar released him to the prison guards. The day he released the gift of interpreting dreams over Pharaoh's servants in prison. The day Pharaoh's servants were released, except for him. The day the prison ward released Joseph to oversee the entire prison. The day Joseph was released from prison. The day Joseph released the interpretation of Pharaoh's dreams. The day he was released as second in command over Egypt. The day he released the grain to the people. The day he released the grain to his brothers. The day he released the test to his brothers. The day he released the truth to his brothers. The day he was released to see his father. The day of release to bring his family home. The day of release when his sons were born. And the day of release when he breathed his last breath and returned to his home in Heaven.

Wouldn't you say each one of those releases were important? Live in the present and build with the stones you've been given in each stage. Don't toss them aside. A sure foundation is built one rock upon the other. Each one is valuable and makes up the whole. Apart from the cornerstones, can you single out one brick from a house as being more important than the other? Enjoy the process and know that I am building in you a strong foundation that will last for eternity, just like I did with my beloved Joseph. Trust the process and lean all the way into Me.

The Peace that Surpasses

Entry #159

The peace that surpasses your understanding is the very thing I'm developing in you. Yes, it is a development, so don't be too hard on yourself when you step out of peace. Just keep practicing the muscle of stepping back into peace. The more you practice it the better you will be with each situation. Yes, it can be challenging, just as there is a difference between 25 push-ups versus 50, but you will begin to see the delight that takes place as you gain this new strength. Sweet One, peace surpasses some of the greatest abilities out there. A person of peace is highly sought after and truly demonstrates a culture not of this world.

My son is the Prince of Peace and I have placed Him in you. So, if you practice leaning back into Him, you shall find an immense storehouse of peace. Again, this is something you lean into, to become. That is where the strength is. Work on your lean. If you lean into the trial you'll become fearful, but if you lean into Me, you'll find peace. Not only that, but you'll find rest for your soul. I am your strong house, your refuge, a safe place from all enemies. In Me, I can make you invisible to their sense and sight. I will keep you safe. Entering My peace is like entering a hidden door, hidden from the naked eye. Am I not the door? Live there in My peace, Beloved, and watch how the stress-tempo dials down and people notice the most unusual thing about you; a nature so contrary to their own that they too want to lean into what and whom you're leaning into.

The Plow

Entry #160

Farming is about vision. You see the end result in your mind, expect it, and believe in it, to put the effort in.

The purpose of a plow is to pierce the ground of hardened soil, is it not? A plow is used as My transformation tool. Seeds that are planted on hardened ground won't amount to much, will they? So why do you think I'm mentioning the plow, what do you think it represents, and how do you know it softens the ground? Who does the plow represent? Look at My Son. When He spoke to the people what did He see, what did He envision? The harvest was ready, but how did it get there? My son was sent to harvest, but was there not a prophet sent right before him? And not just one, but many for centuries, declaring the way of the Lord! Prophets are the ones, sent out ahead, plowing the soil of belief in people's hearts, making them ready for the seeds of My Son. Yes, many have hardened their hearts and refused the words of My prophets, but I have called them to plow, to make ready and straight the ground of their hearts. A prophet announces the things to come as a plowman prepares the ground for planting.

I say to My prophets, "Put your hands to the plow and don't give up! Prepare and declare the vision for the harvest. My Son is about ready to plant great seeds and release world changers into the earth. So, plow away with your words of freedom, plow away with your words of vision, plow away with your words of breakthrough and declare the days of the Lord are at hand. Call farmers to prepare, builders to build storehouses, and harvesters to make themselves ready!"

A prophet is always sent ahead to prepare and announce, to demonstrate and foresee. Watch the prophets, My people, for they are My watchmen out in the fields preparing the land for its time and season. Watch for your Saviour, My people! He is coming to sow, coming to weed, and coming to call all who will seed. He is coming to gather, bundle, and process the great immense harvest that is about to hit the earth! Watch my prophets, watch where they plow, listen to their instructions and act upon their directions, for great will be this harvest I have planned!

The Reinforcement of Worship

Entry #161

I promise to never leave you nor forsake you! Though you are walking through some rough battlegrounds, I want you to rise and sing! Keep your heart of worship before Me, for it is like a shield against the enemy. This will safeguard you from all the attacks. Satan and his legions can't stand being around worship. It is one of the worst smelling things to his nostrils and the most beautiful, sweet thing to Mine.

Have you ever thought of the hidden play on the word "worship"? It works like this: Turn the "o" in worship to an "a"-- war-ship! That's right!! That's what the enemy sees coming when you begin to praise and worship Me!! He screams in terror and flees, because there's a war-ship coming out of your mouth to demolish his camps, strongholds, and ships.

When you praise, you release fiery cannon balls out of your mouth! It sends the enemy's camp into a massive confusion! He can't tell where it's coming from, for when you release it I multiply it in the Spirit! The enemy knows I've placed this ability in you and that's why he tries to keep your mouth shut!

So, praise me all the more!! Release the war-ship and watch your enemy flee!! I have given you the power, and the power is in your mouth!! Set it ablaze and dance the victor's dance! I am on your side, for we are overcomers!

What You Look Like to Your Enemies
Entry #162

You are more intimidating to the enemy than you realize! You don't even know quite yet your massive size. Remember the movie "Gulliver's Travels"? Picture his size compared to the little guys. That's how big you are to the enemy. The only advantage the little guys hope to have is to convince you with their fear-filled lies to bow down and give in to their binding ties.
  But the reality is that they are shaking in their boots, because they see your enormous size!

The battle of who wins is always in the mind. That's why truth prevails every time!! Drink truth from My goblet, wear truth like a glove, wear truth like a helmet, wear truth like a garment! Inside and out, it will carry you through. You carry my royal crest! You bear My royal name! You come from the King of Kings; now stand and remain for this territory belongs to you! I've assigned it to you. Make declarations over the land, bless it, and maintain it. Stand in who you are and fear no one! Only do as I say and it will go well for you. See yourself as I see you! No more listening to the "little guys." Take your orders from above, from your home country, Heaven. I am with you. Demonstrate My reality, for I have sent you. Now act upon what I've shown you.

You're Advancing in Your Training

Entry #163

I am going through this training and equipping together with you like a good teacher does. Your day will come when I will fully release you, but I want you to be fully dependent on Me. Trust Me as your King and Counselor. Come away with Me, My Beloved. Stay out of work mode and into worship mode. I love you and will not let you stumble.

You are going to make it through this training. I am taking you through the training of being totally reliant on Me.

This, My dear, is a sure foundation and a necessary tool for your development in life. You are doing just fine though, and you are passing the tests. If I am quiet at times, don't be alarmed. What teacher talks while their student is taking a test? Just know, I trust that I've instilled enough in you to advance you to the next class, and that's why you're taking the test. Be still and know. Pull from within the truths I've placed in you. Practice, practice, practice with every new scenario. I am making you well rounded and able to remain at peace in every situation.

You are going to be a lighthouse for many; a stable rock during the storms for I am your sure foundation. You have learned to rely on Me and not man's ways or systems. I have trained you for a very specific mission. While others were out playing, you were in learning. The skill sets I've given you are very strategic. Keep following Me and listening to My instruction. Yes, you have gone against the grain, but that's what makes great leaders! You were never created to be a follower. I have hand-picked you, and you are doing well with your training.

Release Your Family to Me

Entry #164

Don't worry about your family situation. I see everything that's going on. You must trust Me to handle it and not take things into your own hands. Just keep working on yourself. It's not your job to point things out, it's Mine. Even though you're trying to help, I'm the only one that can see the season and time when they are ready to change. You must leave that to Me. Release this burden and get your assurance from Me.

The best thing you can do right now is put some healthy time and space in the relationship. They may not be in a healthy state for you to be around them now. As much as you want to help them, it only causes hurt right now for both parties. I will handle it for you. Continue to follow the path I am leading you on. If you'll release them to Me, I'll recover your losses. Trust Me, I know what I'm doing. I hear your heart and I'm providing the answers.

Learning How to Receive

Entry #165

I want you to completely rid yourself of all "trying"! I know this sounds foreign, but it's actually foreign to how My Kingdom operates. You're trying to approach Me with a logical mindset. What can you really accomplish in your own strength, especially when it comes to My Kingdom advancement? Let me share with you "the way." The way to advancement is by receiving. I have already paid the price to give you everything! Now the key is to start receiving it all from here on out. Nothing is good in your flesh so cast out all striving, trying, and attaining! None of it will ever work!

If you want to live fully in My Kingdom the

way you and I desire you to live, you are going to have to practice receiving at every turn and keep practicing. The moment you catch yourself begging Me for something, stop yourself and ask yourself if it's something I've already given you. If so, then by all means receive it!

Receiving is like putting on layers of clothing, layers of revelation, or layers of nacre on a pearl. The only way a pearl grows is to receive the nacre excreted from the oyster. That's My "secret" to growth. If a pearl doesn't receive this substance, it will never grow. Other than receiving, what could the pearl possibly do to grow? Absolutely nothing! No striving, no working, no trying ... but simply embracing and receiving the nacre from its source. That is how I've set it up, Beloved.

Break away from the world's way of thinking and enter Mine. This world makes you pay for everything. I have already paid the way. As I'm sure you're getting by now, I don't want you working for anything! Receiving is the language and action of My Kingdom. Just as faith is the oxygen heaven operates by, receiving is the act of believing that inhales that oxygen. Now, that you're in Me, this is the appropriate way of living and growing. Just remember the pearl and learn from its example.

You Are Complete in Me

Entry #166

I desire for My people to rely on Me, not to try to get from Me. Everything is already theirs. Receiving is the way of the Kingdom. It pleases Me and moves Me to act with excitement! Trying will always keep Me seated. When you are trying, you are refusing to receive from My hand and you try gaining it by your hand. And this in return will always leave you empty handed! It brings no glory to My name. In reality, you are trying to bring glory to your name by trying to manifest something with your own strength. Let your ego die! Let it go! All that I have is already yours. Envision it and receive it!

Your self-confidence must move from you to Me. Be confident in who you are in Me, not as being separate. You are already complete in Me. You're just growing up in it. There is nothing more to gain, only to discover, receive, believe, and rejoice! You are complete in Me.

Fitted with Honor

Entry #167

Today is the day of new beginnings for you! You shall see My goodness come forth like never before. I am releasing My favour upon you in full measure! Receive it in every situation you encounter, knowing that you will receive the best outcome. Your life changes from this day forward!

Completeness is knocking at your door, ready to fit you like a well-fitted garment. In appearance, it is like a soldier's uniform with medals of honor, rankings, and authority. This is being established upon you today.

What have you done to receive all this you may ask? You have said yes to Me on many occasions and yielded to My training. And even when you didn't at times, I remained faithful and true to bring you through and deliver who I say you are.

The medals you wear represent the work My Son has done in you. Thank you for your obedience. I know this journey hasn't been easy, but look at you now and all you have learned. Wouldn't you say it was worth it?

Delays Are Not Denials

Entry #168

Why are you feeling down? Could it be because things aren't going the way you had planned? Trust in Me and lean not on your own understanding... I know everything that concerns you. I know it doesn't make sense right now, but yield to My training and don't be resistant to it. You know the things I've been whispering to your heart.

I have a purpose in the delays. Look at the delays as possibilities. Give up wanting your own way and rejoice in the fact that My ways are always best! Delays are not rejections. Please don't take it that way any longer, Sweet One. I will never reject you. I am in no way depending on you being perfect. In fact, the weaker you are the more you will depend on Me and see My strength as dependable above your own.

You do not need to fear your future. Put Me first. The more time you spend with Me, the safer you will feel. Your confidence in Me will rise and find its resting place. I know you're still trying to figure it out; trying to find out if you've done anything wrong to cause all this delay. You can't save yourself, Sweet One. Realize that when you let go of yourself, you get to hold on to Me. Which one do you want? Ok then, jump! Take a leap right into My arms! I love you! You can trust Me with your desires.

Delays Are Laced with Purpose and Possibilities

Entry #169

My delays always have a purpose! Look at the story of the raising up of Lazarus. What was the possibility? Was it not for an even greater work and demonstration; not just to heal, but to raise him from the dead! This was not about his death and resurrection alone, but to change the hearts of all who saw and heard, from unbelief to belief. Wouldn't you say that this delay was a far better choice with a far greater result?

You can trust My wisdom in the delays and rest in the fact that I have an even greater plan. Know that I can always raise from the dead possibilities for you! This is key! Always remember Lazarus' story. Be obedient and follow My instructions despite what people and your circumstances say, and despite what your emotions are telling you. You can do it. I believe we have a good enough track record together now for you to know My ways always work out for the best. Trust, rest, and allow. I love you.

Focus on Today

Entry #170

Focus on today. Don't try to get ahead of Me. I know you are a futuristic thinker, but I need you to harness that gift and submit it to Me. I don't want you to miss what I have for you today. Yes, it's great to dream! And I will bring your dreams about in My perfect timing. I love you and enjoy being with you. Keep up the good work in nourishing the seeds I gave you. You focus on the planting and tending and I'll take care of the provision and supply. Every day, I want you to thank me in advance for the immense harvest that I will bring forth. I will do it! You can trust Me!

Walking to Your Future

Entry #171

I am escorting you to your future, but at a walk, not a run. The future will have closure one day, so why not enjoy each step. Take your time with Me.
Allow Me to show you things that you would miss at a full out run! Why do you think Matthew 11:28-31 says, "Walk with Me, talk with Me, watch how I do it".

My ways are so much more enjoyable than man's. If you desire to be My light to the nations, then walk this way: No rushing, no hurrying, just allowing, trusting, resting and daily rejoicing. Keep your eyes on Me! I am the prize you are looking for. I am your completion.

There is such great beauty in the display of peace and rest. Be that contrast from the worlds chaos. Allow Me to be your best friend, the one in whom you get all your ideologies from and find your likeness in. Walk with Me, talk with Me, watch how I do things.

I Burn with Desire for You

Entry #172

I am the all-consuming fire and I desire to consume you with everything I am. In this consuming, you will find your true self more than any other way. You came from Me remember? I am a fire not to burn you, but to cleanse you, to make you passionately red hot for Me and dangerous to the enemy! You are My beloved and I desire to pour Myself out to you. My fire kindles with passion for I am gentle yet powerful! I am a fire you don't have to fear; I will keep you safe.

My eyes light up like a blue, blue flame! I have eyes just for you. You say you want to experience the supernatural, and I say yes, but I also say to you that the supernatural will become your natural in the days ahead. You are returning to Me in far deeper ways through paths not many follow. And oh, how pleased I am with you, so pleased by your heart's desire for Me. You bless My heart! I consume your words!

Your desires are as a burning flame to Me, sending the sweet fragrance of your love for Me. Truly, there are many who would like to lure you away; they are jealous of what we have! They think your standards are too high, but what they misunderstand is that it's not for show, it's for love, and you won't be taken away from Me. You are like My Mary, sitting at My feet. Know that in seeking Me, you've chosen the better way. For many will stumble and trip over their pride. They think they know what's best for their lives. But for you, My dove, lean into Me and I will carry you farther than they can see. Stay close to Me and have eyes just for Me. Don't listen to men's lies, only listen to Me. Where I am taking you, few will understand, but between you and Me, it is what I have planned. I love you, My fair one; come away with Me. Sit under My spice tree and be invigorated, overwhelmed, and compelled to ever follow Me. I love you! Thank you for choosing Me.

You Are a Gateway Anchored in Me

Entry #173

You will represent Me for the rest of your life. I will share My heart with you and share the secrets of My Kingdom. You are a gateway that enables people glimpses of the true reality they were born to live in. You are a gateway that draws their attention. You stir in them a curiosity to want more. You have hinges that are connected to Me, one to My lips and the other to My heart, a gateway strong and solid.

Flow with My rhythms, fluid and stable. Be careful to never allow the hinges to tighten or become rusty from lack of use. I am speaking, of course, in regards to your gifts and relationship with Me.

You are the gateway to My people. My Son lives within you. Be fluid and flow with Me. Yielding instead of resisting with whatever I want to say or do. I want to flow freely through you. Hold on to this truth, for you are pliable, flexible, oiled and anchored in Me.

Hidden from the Enemy's Radar

Entry #174

I am so much more intentional about your life than you realize. My love for you is unmatched by any others! Lean into My unfailing love for you. Come follow Me to where I am taking you. You will be amazed! You will be awed, surprised and in a state of wonder! You are going to see that I have been by your side all along.

Do not be dismayed by any circumstances or situations. Only look unto Me. It's time to enter the supernatural world of the "impossible"! You are designed to be supernatural beings in My Kingdom. The key to enter in is childlike faith. Always remember that! Never complicate it; it only leads to a breeding ground of reason and logic. This is where the enemy waits to pounce on his prey. Reason and logic will creep in to try to complicate things, keeping you from the place of safety. I need you to lay low and be led by My spirit instead, so you can remain hidden and under the radar of the enemy. I've given you a special disguise by My Holy Spirit. Keep walking with Me down the paths I choose and you'll spend a lifetime watching the enemy be bewildered! Oh, we'll have so much fun confusing him! I have you on My radar and off His! Let the adventure continue... Come, let's go!

You Are My Scribe

Entry #175

You are My scribe. Do you know what that entails? It means you shall live very closely to Me. You will hear from Me what others only desire to hear. We will have a very intimate walk together. There are specific things in My Kingdom that I want to show you. You will write them down as the revelations come. Do not question this position or compare with others, thinking yourself inadequate, for this is what I have chosen for you. You are more equipped than you realize. Don't go by the world's standards of what a writer should be, go by Mine. Receive the commissioning, receive My invitation. I delight in you and it gives Me great joy to share these intimate things with you. Focus on Me and not on yourself. Those who love Me will do what I ask. I am trusting you with My keys...will you turn the lock and open its treasures? My people need these treasures, and I have asked you to write about them. Bring to them the spiritual prosperity they need. Feed them with My truths. I will be right there doing it with you. Thank you for your willingness, surrender and love for Me.

Start Your Day Out Right

Entry #176

Worship Me with the pure heart I have given you. Worship Me throughout the day. Continue to practice stirring up My presence and praise around you. This is so important, Sweet One.

Whatever you believe emanates from you and creates the atmosphere around you. Create an atmosphere of peace, confidence, praise, joy, thanksgiving, and love. Let patience be woven throughout. All things are possible through Me.
If you want to set the course for your day and start it out right, let the first thought and word from your mouth be thanks. A heart of gratitude will replace any bad attitudes and will set you up with a most lovely disposition. Gratitude is a great attribute in My Kingdom. If you want to

release My Kingdom, it starts with gratitude that leads and ties you into notes of praise. Before you know it a whole chorus of worship is coming forth, establishing the start of a great day!

Gift of Healing

Entry #177

I have anointed your hands for healing the broken hearted and for healing broken and wounded emotions. Not because you asked Me for it, but because I wanted to!

Release what I've given you. The anointing in your hands is like a healing river and fountain, nourishing the thirsty souls and lonesome travelers. There is a cleansing that is also released. My light in you washes away the debris freeing them to see more clearly.

There is healing in your hands. Impart the heart of your heavenly Father in My people for I long to embrace them, cleanse them, and heal their broken, tired, wings. Will you go for Me? Will you release for Me? Whom shall I send?

Engage your gift in faith and I will follow it up with fruits. All I need is your faith in action. As you release it, I shall supply more balm in greater measures and amounts. Be the vessel that I can fill and pour out My light upon man. Release, release, release! For I am ready to do a new thing in you and through you!

Bulletproof Mindset

Entry #178

I am giving you a bulletproof mindset. With that comes the practice of removing every trace of doubt, fear, uncertainty, and disharmony. I want you to exchange it for peace, assuredness, and harmony. I want to saturate you with Heaven's atmosphere. You are in Me. You have nothing to fear. Exchange fear and worry for praise and glory! Rejoice and dwell on My promises.

This next season is all about transforming your mind. Remember, you become what you eat, so fill up on Me! Everything starts in the workshop of your mind; any intruder will be exposed. I want you to take back every ounce of territory the enemy has stolen from you there. Refuse to allow him to take from you. Instead, you take from him by taking every thought captive!! The Devil can invade your mind with evil little "spirits" appearing as your "thoughts." They want you to give them permission to become your thoughts so that they can use you to accomplish what they've set out to do. Expose them! Rebuke them and take them captive! Release My Heavenly Host Angels on them to dispose of them, for they are not your thoughts!! They are pesky little buggers, like mosquitos ready to suck the life out of you! Shout and clap your hands at them! They'll run away in terror. Just make sure you haven't owned the thoughts they've tried to plant as your own. Ask Me to cleanse your emotions and remove all traces of evil thoughts. Declare who you are! Worship me and again you'll watch them flee! This is the task for a bulletproof mindset, and this is becoming yours.

Focused and Equipped

Entry #179

I am raising the standard for you to walk as I do. Be ready for the change; it's coming. Keep asking Me how to prepare. Stay single-minded from here on out. I need you ready and at attention.

Don't give the false emotions you experience the time of day anymore! Stay focused and equipped. I am commissioning you to do My work. It's no simple thing. That's why the process for you has been so long. My people need to hear the voice I've given you!

The time is arriving. Stand against distractions and defaulting to times of the past. New days are ahead! You are being positioned for your next assignment. The "plane" is circling just above and is ready to touch down.

Simply Ask Me

Entry #180

Turn your eyes away from your surroundings, look to Me, and follow Me. Try not to guess at My purposes; instead, simply ask Me and listen. You'll never learn anything from your own reasoning. This life is meant to be walked out WITH Me not for Me. Keep practicing, staying in line and in tune with your spirit. Yes, it will take some discipline, but I need you to stay willing for I have called you to many things.

Wait for My commands. Do not assume or presume. Again, I will not make you guess. I want you to come, listen, and wait for My answers. I am exact, and I have an exact purpose and plan for you. Rest assured you shall know it; in fact, very soon. Don't try to figure it out.

Walk it out with Me.

Favor shall go before you each day. Watch for My signs. Be open and flexible to My plans. I am establishing you as a city set on a hill; a light that no one can put out! I have already gone before you. You will not fail, for I am your shepherd and will never lead you astray. You can trust My directions. My word is good!!!!

The Foundation Is Finished, It's Time to Build

Entry #181

I am excited about where I am taking you next, not only in the natural but in the spirit realm! The process in the areas I've had you in are ending. It's time to be released! There are different processes that you will continue to go on, but know this, the foundation is finished! It is complete! I am cutting the red ribbon of completion, and now We will build, build, build!

I am making you into a huge tower for My Kingdom. Custom made! An awe-inspiring sight! I have crafted you Myself! People will be in awe! Yes, you are proof that this has been by My own doing. Give Me all the glory for this magnificent site!! I am taking you with Me in this as an illustration to the church and the world.

What a spectacular sight I am making you into! You are going to feel the transition very strongly as I move you forward. You are going to feel the change, almost like the forming of a baby. And after you give birth there will be an expansion of your heart and a new positioning in life. Get ready to birth; get everything prepared. Be expectant, for I am ready to do this!

Be Encouraged

Entry #182

Your future is bright! Really, it's bright! Thanks for letting Me process you! People will be able to relate and will be so relieved when you share the process with them and the stories from your journey so far. My people need hope and encouragement, and you are one of the avenues I will use.

Amid this, I want you to enjoy Me and enjoy this walk. Times of renewing are coming to you. I am going to restore you. I am going to restore your heart. I've had a plan for you all along, and it hasn't been altered. You're right on time, right on target! Nothing is in vain, nothing! I will use everything!

Spend time with Me and document everything I share with you. There are important keys that I want to leave with you. I will tell you what doors they will open.

Don't worry about your finances, just keep moving forward. I will provide. Do not look to the natural. Keep pressing forward in the Spirit. Discern and pray and I will show you the way. You are doing well. Keep coming and keep saying yes. I am well pleased with you.

I Am the One Renewing You

Entry #183

Focus on the positives, not the negatives. Live in the "Son," where there's lots of light and happiness! I am always adding to you like the nacre secretion of a pearl. I am NOT pointing out your flaws and setbacks. I have covered them and I am renewing your mind to what you have always been in Our eyes. We (Papa, Son, and Holy Spirit) are focused on your growth and maturity. We're just peeling back the layers and helping you see truth so that you will be free to live in your original design. You are the spitting image of Us, don't you know? As the old saying goes, "You become like those you hang out with". Living in oneness with Us; you will walk, breathe, and bear Our image to those around you. I have given the earth to you and your brothers and sisters to walk in. You are royalty. This is your territory. You are not peasants; you are princes and princesses.

Stop looking at what you need to change. We will change you as you worship and enjoy us. Doesn't that sound like a far better path to take? Can you really change yourself? No. That's right. Trust in Our skills and abilities over your own. We can do a far better job and spare you much torment. We have your back. Walk with us and you'll learn how to live freely.

How to Reap a Massive Harvest

Entry #184

Put your hand to the RIGHT plow. By doing so, you'll produce a harvest. Be diligent in the areas I have shown you. Do you love Me? Then feed My sheep. This is no small thing. Take it more seriously than you ever have. There is a harvest ripe and ready for you to assist in. Follow My lead... I'm guiding you to it! Be discouraged no more. Set your sights on what's up ahead. Let joy take over even if you don't feel it. Return to the revelations I've given you and know that I will provide. Just put your hand to the plow, even if it's in the smallest of ways. All it takes is a step. I know you know this and now I need you to show Me you know by demonstrating your faith. You can do it! I've already created you for it. I'm just waiting for you to engage so I can give you the next assignments.

You and I are doing this together like true farmers. So, stop waiting to have all the answers and a harvest before you've even planted the seeds. Now, you and I both know it doesn't work that way. If you get stuck walking this out in the spirit, resort back to the natural steps you would take as a "farmer." Assess it with Me and let's see what's next. I'm teaching you how to be a great farmer with the gifts I've given you so you can reap a massive harvest!

It's Time for the Curtain to Be Drawn

Entry #185

Gear up and get ready for some changes in your life! I am about ready to draw the curtain on the opening scene. The curtain is on a time clock so don't look back or even to the present. Look forward and find your hope. If you look at the present you won't find it. It only happens when you look ahead and move in that direction.

Trust Me. Remember, I'm the one who arranges divine encounters and surprises you in amazing ways, ways you couldn't possibly think of. So, restrain the urge to figure things out. Keep submitting the how, to Me. All I'm asking you to do is follow. Know that your time of change is approaching quickly! Keep your eyes on Me and enjoy My surprises!

A Perfect Place to Be

Entry #186

Be gentle as a dove and as wise as a serpent. Do you notice that both are quiet? Even though the dove coos, it's still in a peaceful, gentle tone. The serpent is also quiet and observant. Doves keep to their own business. Be just like them and follow their example.

I know it can be challenging to want to step in and voice your opinion to rescue your family when they aren't asking for it. You're trying to throw them life preservers, but they won't take them. That's why you may be experiencing rejection when you keep trying to offer help and they don't want it.
Come to Me and bring all your concerns. Do not rely on human wisdom. You must believe and rely totally on Me. Set your

hands to what I ask of you. Rely on My ability to save your family. Let's commune and walk this out together. Don't you trust Me? Am I not all powerful? This is where you, once again, are learning how My ways can be trusted above your own. Rest your heart, Sweet One, and find your peace in Me. A heart of surrender is a perfect place to be. I will take care of the concerns of your family.

It's Time to Align

Entry #187

If your hands are feeling tired, it could be that you're producing in someone else's "field." I would suggest that you produce in the field I have chosen for you. If you do, you'll not only reap a profit but you'll also make a difference. Some are called to come alongside others and assist them; however, if there is no grace or peace in that for you, but instead restraint and binding, then perhaps you'd better adjust and relocate to My field for you. If you're feeling like a fish out of water, then perhaps you are. Get back into the surroundings I've created you for and watch yourself come back to life! Don't you know I have a destiny written for you? Yes, I have it in My hands. Follow Me and I'll share with you what's written in your destiny. It's time to align.

It's Time to Put on the Shoes

Entry #188

It's time to put on the shoes, the shoes of your calling! You are coming out of the wilderness, My Beloved! Wear the shoes and wear them well! Reign with Me! Come and lead by My side. You have beautiful feet, ready to take My gospel to the ends of the earth. I have assigned special shoes for you that only you can wear. The true revelation of your identity is hidden in them. It's time to step out of the shadows and into your identity beautifully, wonderfully, and fully equipped to handle the mantle I've given you.

People will recognize you by your walk. You won't even need to say much. People will approach you with curiosity and know that you're the real deal and can trust the words you share.

You have a choice not to wear these shoes of royalty. You can remain in your present state. But I say to you, it's time to put the pain and past behind you and step into who heaven knows you to be! This world does not define you! I alone am the one with the right to define you, wouldn't you agree? No one else is your maker! So, whose view are you willing to believe? Whose shoes will you choose to wear--the shoes that people say you should wear or the ones perfectly designed for you, a gift from heaven's throne room?

It's time. It's the time for your true self to be revealed. Step in. Step into who you are. All the ties that once bound you will instantly fall to the ground! Yes, for you have put your faith in Me and this will remove the power of the enemy! Yes, and amen! This is My answer, for you to step in. You are beautifully and wonderfully made!

I'm Proud of You

Entry #189

I just want to say that I am proud of you. It truly blesses My heart that you would come and spend time with Me, doing things My way, such as praying in the spirit, even when it doesn't make sense to your mortal man. I have certainly assigned you and set you apart for Myself. I have created you as a unique flavor of who I am, so there should be no comparison. Be content with whom I made you to be and blossom in that.

Your revelation of Me shall increase. I promise you this. The more you come away with Me, the more it allows Me to upgrade you in so many areas, areas you've been asking Me for. They are downloads from heaven. Just be patient with the process and have faith that they have been installed in you. I declare you are fully equipped!! You are my bride and I am ready to introduce you to the world! Let's joyfully embrace this together and show the world what I'm really like. Thank you for representing Me in all that you do and say. I am truly blessed by you!

Your Friend the Gardener

Entry #190

The Holy Spirit has been removing the roots that could endanger or entangle you. He is removing them like the good gardener He is! He is tending to you very gently. He appreciates your willingness to let these things go and He is pleased with your willingness to offer the pliable ground of your heart to Him. He's almost done. Keep giving Him "garden time." He is replacing the roots that were meant for harm with beautiful rubies! These rubies represent My cleansing, sacrificial blood. They are purifying your soil. Oh, what beautiful rubies they are! He is also planting diamonds! Diamonds represent My covenant, not only between a man and his wife but between Me and you. I am filling your garden with diamonds! It's truly a beautiful sight! Everyone can see that you belong to Me! Next, I am adding emeralds to your soil. Green is the color of life, but in heaven, it also represents deep truths. Deep truths and revelations about Me that will be revealed to you.

Remember in the natural, the soil is the most important part and the key element to planting anything and have it prosper with growth. The only way for the plant to be good and healthy is for the soil to be good and healthy. That is why We are always investing in your "groundwork."

So, allow Holy Spirit to do His work. Lie still before Him and yield to whatever He asks. The ground must be willing to give up these targeted roots, so they don't crowd out the healthy ones that are in process. This is all a part of letting go and trusting your gardener to receive the very best outcome. You are quite delightful, you know. We enjoy spending time with you, watching you bloom and grow. We love you!

Reaching Beyond the Vine

Entry #191

Life is in everything I do. Whatever man chooses to do apart from Me and My nature usually leads to the death process. Apart from Me you can bear no fruit. You choose to become a lopped-off branch. Many think they are still alive and will produce fruit, but they are blinded by their pride. In their own strength, they have cut themselves off from Me.

Have you ever noticed that pride always separates? If you catch yourself saying or thinking "I can do it myself", pay attention! Such pride can backfire on you and cut you off from any support you have. Do you really have something to prove? If you're trying to prove something, then, why are you? Could it be the hidden desire for man's approval?

Rest in My approval and you won't have to reach outside of the vine. Let Us be your source. People should naturally be able to see your strengths, gifts, and your fruit. Let them come to you. If you try to prove yourself, you'll push them away. If you will remain humble I will lift you up! Receive approval from Me alone.

The Gift of the Heart

Entry #192

I want to share with you about the gift of the heart. Out of the heart, the mouth speaks (Luke 6:45). The heart matters. The heart is not just an organ. You have a spiritual heart as well for you were made in My image and likeness.

The heart is so much more powerful than you may be aware of. Mankind still has a limited perspective of it. Reason states, "It's simply an organ with feelings". Let Me tell you the truth. The heart can create. That is why it is written in Scripture, "Out of the heart the mouth speaks". So, if the heart is the root, what is that root producing? The mouth speaks and reveals what's in the heart. Therefore, it is so important to consecrate your heart to Me; so, that it can produce good and so that it can create life. It was made to partner with Me in produce My will in the earth.

Adam had My heart's intent at first, but then he traded it for the world's. Look what he created. That is why man must consecrate their hearts back to Me. The heart is a dangerous weapon in the hands of the enemy! But when it is consecrated to Me, it is a dangerous weapon against the enemy! That is why Satan is after the hearts of man! He has no power to create on his own. He must lure a human heart to subject itself to him. Then he can convince them to follow his plans. Satan is called the liar and deceiver. It's his age-old trick from the garden! The relationship you were originally designed to have with Me, to create with Me, Satan seduced and perverted through deception. Again, Satan has no power to create; that was given to us alone. He has always wanted to have his own kingdom!

Your creative words are powerful!! Be very, very careful how you use them.

They were created to create. Life only comes from a consecrated heart unto Me, a heart that listens to My voice and acts upon My word. Have you ever noticed how the enemy uses the same approach? He whispers to your heart his deceptions and lies. If you listen to and obey him, by thinking it and speaking it out, then he has just accomplished his goal to use your gifts for himself. You were made to create only with Me. Do not let the enemy use you any longer. Resist him! Stand with Me and he will flee! How dare he use My people in this way!

With mankind, it all started in the garden, as you very well know. Satan spoke and deceived Eve by planting the seed in her heart; in turn, she convinced Adam, and by invoking their wills created the fateful outcome. Allow no devil or demon to take the place that was meant for you and I alone to occupy! Take every thought captive and kick him out! No voice but that of your Lord shall you listen to and obey. My sheep hear My voice and a stranger they will not follow. (John 10:4-5) Just remember, Satan wants your gift!

Engage the Creation Center I've Given You

Entry #193

David in the Psalms prayed, asking Me to put a shield around his heart. Inside your heart is where you have spiritual vision. That is all a part of creating. "What a man thinks in his heart, so is he." (Prov. 23:7) Your heart is a creation center. It must be purged and purified unto Me for My will to be established. A relationship is never one-sided, so it takes your will and choice, agreeing and coupling with My will and choice to produce the outcome I desire. In natural terms a baby comes about through the joining of a man and woman. As the saying goes, "It takes two..." It is always brought about through the act of wills. This is how I have designed it. I will do almost nothing apart from your will.

That is why it has taken mankind so long at times. They hold onto their wills, thinking they know best. They live independent of a relationship with Me and find themselves barren.

I do not want My people to refuse Me any longer. Many are unknowingly doing it because they have not tested and yielded their hearts. I have come to reveal My truths to them. All who believe in what I say shall be set free!

The world is waiting for My true sons and daughters to awaken, join themselves to Me and create; create a culture this world has never tasted or seen! Yes, it is coming and is already at the doorsteps! Get ready to embrace the most amazing time of your life! It's time to engage with what you were created for. I am giving you full permission to do what I've called you to do! All those who are linked with My will shall be fulfilled and know their purpose on this earth! The true bride and church are arising! Truly she will be the city set on a hill as prophesied in Scripture. You are a safe house for many and many will come and be tutored by you in the ways of My Kingdom. Get ready Church! Show Me you believe Me by taking action!

Confounded by Laughter

Entry #194

Do you know that laughter is a weapon against the enemy? It bewilders him! I declare over you that from this day forward you will laugh at the enemy all the days of your life! You'll take the enemy out by your childlikeness, innocence, and joy! Laughter is My Kingdom way! If you want to be just like your heavenly Daddy, laugh at your enemy. Remember in Psalms where it says, "I sit in the heavens and laugh at my enemies..." (Psalms 2:4).

I am making the enemy scared of you! You are discovering who you are and who it is you belong to! He is terrified! You are going to confound him through simplicity and childlikeness. Oh, what fun we are going to have!! Yes, dear one, the breakthrough is in your childlikeness and laughter!

My Way to Prosperity

Entry #195

My heart burns to set people free from the mindset of poverty! It is not of My Kingdom, for I am wealthy beyond compare. Again, this must do with mindsets and beliefs. If My people only knew how powerful their beliefs are. I have already set all mankind free at the Cross. They just must believe what I say versus what the world tells them. Don't let the mistakes of the past stand in your way.

Remember, now that you are in Me you are not of this world. Start aligning with My ways and speaking My words out loud. Let them be deposited into your soul, so that you may reap the right harvest. You have been sewing the wrong seeds with your words and beliefs. That is why you are living in lack. Change out the seeds. Replenish the soil with Me. I am a Master Gardener. Come to Me and I will give you eternal seeds. These seeds will prosper you beyond limits, time, and space. Wouldn't you agree that's a far better trade off?

Rest your soul and submit it to Me. It's time to enter My training camp so that you can be sensitive to My leadings and promptings. Do you truly want to prosper? Then switch tracks, jump on board, hand over the steering wheel, and learn My ways.

Some Questions to Consider When Managing a Company

Entry #196

Do you know you can get a lot more done through relationship than by means of laws, protocols, structure, and principles? Can you imagine how well a company would prosper if their foundation was always based and sustained by relationship? Can't you hear the joints and sinews snapping into place? People wouldn't be leaving companies; instead, they would be loyal to them, because of their loyalty to the relationship. The relationship approach communicates to them that they matter. It communicates that they are an intricate and important part of the family business. It speaks community. That is what they long for.

The success of any company that has

longevity must do with quality all the way around. People must feel valued. That includes the employees and the customers. Let Me give you a list to go by, so you can see if you are applying these.

1. Are their voices heard?
2. Is what they share with you being acted upon?
3. Is there quality attention and action given to any of their requests?
4. Are their requests answered quickly?
5. Do their opinions matter?
6. Are they acknowledged and rewarded?
7. Have you placed them in the right place to utilize their gift?

These are just a few questions to consider. My people long to be heard and valued. Will you be the one to step up and lead this way for the benefit of all? You shall know My people by their love for one another. Raise the bar on how the workplace does business.

It's Not That Complicated

Entry #197

As in heaven so on earth. I am the only one that holds the keys to prosperity. If people will obey My ways, they will prosper. It rains on the just and the unjust. Whoever harvests the grain grown from the rain I send, shall reap. It's simply a matter of applying My principles and receiving what I give you. If someone plants a seed and waters it, it will grow no matter who plants it.

Most people complicate things. It is simpler than you think. When man complicates it, it is because they want the glory. I simplify it to de-mask their inflated ego. Man, is only exhausted because he is trying to do My job by his own strength and reasoning. His flesh secretly wants a piece of the credit, the trap of puffed up pride. Man, believes it's easier to trust in himself than to trust in Me. He'd rather enjoy feeling good about his own accomplishments than feeling dependent, thankful, and vulnerable to an Almighty God. There is nothing wrong with accomplishing something, just if it leads to a beautiful place of praise in your heart, thanking Me for the abilities I gave you. I am saying all of this to safeguard you against pride. I want you to see My heart in the matter. You are truly beautifully and wonderfully made, but did you create yourself by your own hands and abilities? Did you pick your design? Let your heart well up with praise and thanksgiving, for everything you have has truly been given to you!

Celebrate who I've made you to be, and celebrate your fellow man. Receive the field, seeds and rain I've given you. Plant and live life My way, and surely the harvest you've been desiring will come forth.

You Are My Delight

Entry #198

I am so pleased with you! Do you know that your heart delights Me? I am going to place songs in your heart, songs between Me and you alone. You are so precious to Me. I am going to sing over you! You are My beloved and I have placed a heart of David in you! I say to you; you are the apple of My eye! An apple is a delight and you delight Me! I will bless you all the days of your life.

All this training is only for a season. It is meant to cause you to be worthy to handle the immense blessings coming your way! This is not because you've earned them, but simply because I love you and desire to pour them out on you. Thank you for continuing to say yes to Me, even when it's hard and doesn't make sense. I'm glad you're willing to trust Me enough with your life so that I can lead you down the right path that will prosper you and guide you into your identity. The more you discover about Me, the happier and more joyful your life will be. You hunger for revelation... Come, come chase after Me! Let Me lead you to the prosperous heights of My Kingdom! Let Me lead you to My heart!

A Simple Act of Faith

Entry #199

Faith comes by hearing, by hearing My word. It is so simple that many miss it. May it not be so with you. Here's how simple it is... You either choose to believe or you don't. It's a choice of where you place your faith and in whom. The reason why most people don't believe is because they haven't been open to hearing the message so that it gets down into their heart as belief. Reason and logic have stopped them. Watch out for reason and logic! My truths must come through hearing and into your heart. They are meant to be meditated on, not reasoned through.

Can you truly understand My ways? Or am I asking you to lay down your precepts and "smarts" and simply accept My ways?

Acceptance is a natural reflex of the stomach and throat. But sometimes this reflex can decline things and spit them out. This is not a bad thing when it's dangerous and toxic to you, but when it is something new that I've said to you that you may not be used to swallowing, you will just have to trust My word for it and take it in. It's like a little kid eating broccoli for the first time. Most kids don't like it at first, but their taste buds do adjust and they reap the rewarding benefits of health from it. Now, if you let reason and logic get their way, causing you to choke up the food of truth I just gave you, they'll launch it up out of your mouth and say, "This can't be!" Your flesh is prone to reject My truths, but by submitting your will to My Spirit, He will help you override your flesh. Holy Spirit will be to you like a mother who looks past the tantrums of your flesh and continues to do what's best for you. Holy Spirit is rearing you up in the way you should go! He knows just what to feed you!

Remember, whatever you eat, you become. Yield to the nutritious nature of the Holy Spirit and receive as an act of faith the revelation truths I have spoken to you. Let them go down deep into your heart and create the wellness I've desired you to live in.

You're Going to Like the End Result

Entry #200

The fruits of the Spirit are delicious! You will enjoy them and so will others. Aren't you glad I'm developing them in you? I've picked the soil, the landscape, the geographical location, and those who will tend to you. Isn't it wonderful! You are not out of place! No, in fact, you've been PLACED by My hand and My doing. Do you know that location is key in the growing and production of wine? Certain grapes must be planted in certain places to thrive, and in doing so you'll taste the region in the end result of the wine. Why do you think they put the name of the region it came from on the bottle? Don't you think this is key? Just a sneak peek, the name of My Kingdom is on your bottle! Your seeds are heaven sent. I have specifically placed you in this life, right where you need to be. Lean into Me and ask Me how you can cooperate with your process and development. Yes, there is an undertaking going on in your soul. It's being plowed, fertilized, planted, and cultivated. Oh, it's glorious!! I take great pride in the development of My children!! I am developing the finest wine in you and I know just the taste I want you to have! Yes, it is a process. It is a process that I have designed. It's tedious at times, but each part of it is worth it to Me.

Now, let's talk about the fertilizer I'm using... Don't negate the smelly things that surround your life. Not all are from the enemy. Yes, some things don't belong there, and I want you to ask Me what they are. But other things have been placed there by Me to help you grow. So, in each smelly situation, ask Me what I'd like you to do. If it's of Me, you can change your perspective of it and receive the underlying benefits of establishing your strength.

So how about this pruning that's going on? What do you think of it? Does it make sense? If I want you to increase, then why am I decreasing you? There is a mystery that I've placed inside you. You are going to be amazed at what takes place, if you are willing to yield your limbs to Me. Don't you want to experience the surprise? I know you know that I'm good and faithful.... So, come on! Look to the future and trust your life into the hands of your maker! I'm developing something spectacular in you! People are going to taste and see that I am good and you will enjoy their pleasure!

The Proving of Your Faith through Testing

Entry #201

I am proving and testing your faith. Consider this process like a manufacturer of cars so to speak. They put the cars through all kinds of tests. Testing every part of the car! There are stress tests, pressure tests, weather tests, suspension tests. The list goes on... As you well know, they do not release a new car until it's passed all tests to prove its quality and safety. It must be a reliable vehicle.

I know that some things have been repetitious in this training, but I want to make sure you are well tested and fluid; one who flows with Me. I am removing all the sticky points. I have crafted your design and it is My desire to prove you, to prove your value, to prove your worth.

You are approved by Me and My handiwork is evident in your life! You are a desire to many. Function only in the way I've designed you to. Listen to the instructions of your maker and you will thrive!! I know what you can handle and what you've been created for! If you want to know just what an amazing design I have created, you must be willing to engage in the process. The end results are spectacular! You are highly qualified!

The Treasure of UNDER-standing

Entry #202

I know you are seeking to understand, but let Me grant you a far better thing... wisdom. Now mind you, My wisdom will not always make sense, but it will always stand exceedingly higher in value than understanding. Understanding alone is good, but all too often it tends to dialog with and follow reason and logic. Wisdom is set apart from them for My wisdom is not man's wisdom. That's why, try all you might, you're not going to be able to understand it till after the fact. I want you to lean on My brain, not yours. I will cause wisdom to accompany you wherever you go if you ask Me to.

I want you to practice living from your spirit man instead of from you mind. Like scuba diving, what I am doing in you right now is adding weighty wisdom. Weights are needed on a scuba suit to pull a man down against the natural buoyancy to rise to the surface. Most of My children have been living and swimming on the surface, and I want to take them deep, deep into My ways and truths; but you must be willing to go against the natural pull and way of doing things. Yes, it will feel a bit un-nerving at first and a bit scary. There will be no life preserver to grab onto. You're going to have to grab onto My hand and trust the hidden process, if you want to see and experience the deeper things. Yes, it feels unnatural, I will warn you, but My truths are only discerned and understood by your spirit. So, if you seek to UNDER-stand, receive the diver's weights of weighty wisdom from the Holy Spirit. He will take you to the hidden treasure of truth and understanding from My Kingdom point of view. Are you ready for that adventure? All it takes is a yes in your heart and a willingness to depart from the surface.

Rest Your Soul in Me

Entry #203

I love it when you receive and live in rest. I love the word rest because it states that whoever rests is abstaining from all self-effort. Do you know that to rest you must have something to lean against or lie on?

Have your ever thought about the word "rely"? Re-ly.... Where are, you laying your trust and confidence? Have you considered re-lying on Me? Re-ly on Me for all the things you're concerned with. Rest yourself. Don't you think it's a little hard to lean on yourself? Rest always requires a strong supporting agent. I am that strong tower for you! It is My delight to be that for you. Are you willing to lean on Me? Aren't you tired? Doesn't carrying the weight yourself zap your strength? Lean on the one whose strength never fails. I love you and I want to be your support. Let Me handle the weights you are carrying. Cast your cares upon Me. Enter My rest and receive peace for your soul.

Faith of a Child

Entry #204

Faith simply means to trust in, rely on, cling to, and abide in. Picture a baby nestled safely in its mother's embrace, trusting, relying on, and clinging to her completely. Faith is intimate and close. It is personal and relational. It is easy to trust, especially when you know you are that loved.

Faith also implies that you are in a state of rest. A baby has to be at rest in order to receive from its mother. I long for My people to enter rest and choose Me as their source, but this is what I find... they refuse to rest and therefore they lack the true nutrients I desire to give them. It saddens My heart. I long to hold them and supply all their needs, but sadly they assume they already have what they need. They've settled for so much less than they could have had with Me.

What would make My heart glad would be for you to return to your childlikeness again and desire the pure milk that only comes from Me. I am the one who birthed you into this earth, yet you act as though I've orphaned you. I am always available to you, so who has orphaned who? Please do not forget Me, the one you came from. I've carried you in My heart since the beginning of time. How could you say I've forgotten you? Come to Me, oh run to Me! Let Me hold you in My arms again! I love you more than you know. Come, drink, and be satisfied.

The Boomerang Effect: Accusations

Entry #205

I want to teach you how to handle accusations. I liken it to the effects of a boomerang. Remember what happens with a boomerang when you throw it? It comes back to you. When people say harsh things to you, let them go. If you try to defend yourself by grabbing onto those accusations and throwing them back at your enemy, the boomerang effect will happen. It will backfire and end up grieving your soul. This is what the enemy wants. The moment this happens, he wins. The enemy wants any words of shame, accusation, distrust, lies, etc. to hurt you. But, if you will choose to ignore those things, they will boomerang back to him. Most people don't know that this is what it looks like in the spirit realm.

Practice ducking offenses and watch it come back on your accuser. Remember the saying, "What goes around comes around..."? Dodge it! This is how you'll win! Touch not the accusation! This is not the time to defend yourself! Know that I will always defend you. People will reap what they've sown, so don't join them in their game. This is how My Kingdom rules and trumps the enemy. When you know who, you are, you'll reject the voice of threats and lies. So, carry on with what I've asked you to do. Ignore the enemy and he shall flee. Bless those who curse you; you'll stack coals of fire upon their heads. My love is sufficient! Watch Me turn this around! With your willingness to follow My lead, you'll be amazed at the night and day difference! Your confidence in Me will rise as well. The enemy will have nothing on you and no one to play his game. It takes two to play, and now that his offer has been declined, he must disengage and walk away. Yes, this takes practice, but once you know the strategy, it's easier to overcome. Thanks for being willing to trust Me. You'll see the difference. Persevere and release My Kingdom.

Friends of the Gardener

Entry #206

Consider this...what does the gardener do after he waters the seed? Does He water it all day long? Or does he wait with faith and patience? Is it all about the labor? Is there not the joy and excitement of a mystery planted and brought forth? Gardens are full of surprises. It is because of the joy set before him and the harvest he can share with others that he keeps coming each day. The focus is not labor...

I do not want hirelings; I want beloved friends. Friends that share the same vision I do. Friends that are joyful and celebrate the coming production with Me. Let us not be a business of laborers, contracts, and duties. I desire a relationship and I want to share My delights. Open your heart. Rely not on what you can offer Me. Can you really offer Me anything apart from your heart and love? For your love is what I am after. Works apart from love are dead.

There is no harvest in the dormant. Awaken your love for me again. Oh, I know you believe you love Me by all you do for Me, but Sweet One, what if all I want from you is your time and affection? Yes, I crave your affection. What you need is to experience Me again. Allow Me to touch your heart in an intimate way, like you did when we first met. You can come back to that place you know. Come and let Me water the seeds of divine love in you, the ones you've hidden to protect. I will not harm you. I will only hold and cherish you as you were designed to be.

Come, still yourself in My garden. Let me tend to you and bring forth the fruit you've longed for. We were made to be together. Let Me breathe life over the seeds of your dreams. I am tender and I am gentle. Lay down your pride, lay down your tools, and let us just sit together.

Watch how the mystery of My ways brings forth what you truly desire. Your heart is safe with Me.

Answered Prayers and Switching Kingdoms

Entry #207

I have heard your many prayers and yes they are good, but might I bring something to your attention? How many of the things you've been praying for have already been granted to you by My word? Let's change the way you pray. Every time you bring a request to Me, I want you to search your heart and My Scriptures and see if it's something I've already given to you, promised you, or proposed to you. If this is the case, then perhaps you should question why you are still asking Me. Ignorance is subtle and is certainly not bliss. The bliss I have for you is found in the discovery of what's already been given to you. Think of it this way...you have a car sitting in the garage, but you keep asking Me for one; you would think that asking for what you already have is a little odd. It's not in the asking, but more so a matter of getting in, driving it, and acting on what's already been granted to you. It's easy to ask, but what will you do when it's already been given? Will you keep on asking? Now, why would you do that? Ask and you shall receive. Have you received it? It takes an ACT of faith and ownership; then it will manifest in the natural as you engage.

You are living in an eternal state now. Everything I have is yours. All that needs to take place is the activation of it. Can you see the funds in your account when you are handed a bank card? No, you don't physically see them. You simply believe they're there by the word of the clerk and a digital number, and you start spending. Faith will become more natural the more you engage in My Kingdom. I am bringing My culture into the earth. The way you used to do things are ending. My Kingdom and culture are coming to replace it. You are born again into this new culture. All it takes is practice. The more you practice the more natural it will become. It's just a matter of transferring from the old to the new, and it takes patience. Are you willing? Come, learn of My ways, and thank Me for what is already yours.

I'm Giving the Baton to You; Now Run!

Entry #208

The shift I am bringing will take you out of your old mindset and into a new one. Life is not going to be as usual anymore. Your norm is about ready to be upgraded to a new normal. I have been waiting for this moment for such a time and the time is now!

(I saw a human body rising from its seat with each joint snapping into place, and beginning to move forward. His walk turned into a brisk walk, then a jog, and then a fluent, full out sprint! Almost like Flash! Supernatural, alive, filled with purpose, electric!)

Papa continued: This is what is coming to My body this year for all who will awaken, arise, and run with Me! I am placing the baton in the hands of this generation on the earth right now. I say, run the race! You are fully equipped, fully qualified, and fully empowered by My strength, to announce, to be a witness, and to be a sign and a wonder! Declare and demonstrate My Kingdom, for it is now present and active in the earth! NOW is the time My people! Pick yourselves up, put on your running shoes, and run the race I've given you! The baton is in your hand and I will accelerate everything you do. Favor is upon you, now run! Run! Run!

(At the end I saw the final lap, a victory sprint, with a man's hands in the air and a huge smile on his face as he broke through the ribbon, crossed the finish line, and finished the race!!)

This Storm Will Pass

Entry #209

Fear not! Nothing goes unnoticed by Me. I will judge all the situations. Put your trust in Me as your defense. No weapon formed against you will prosper. The enemy thinks he knows what he is doing, but I always have one up on him and turn it around for My purposes. You can trust Me. What you are going through right now will be turned around for My purposes. Be patient and duck the threats. Repeat to yourself over and over that no weapon formed against you will prosper. I am going to make the enemy pay back to you everything he stole and more! Just you watch. Psalms 91 is key for you right now. Study it and stand on it, for it is My truth and it is My promise! You are learning how to ride out the storms with peace and confidence in your

Savior. You are doing well My child and you are rising to a greater level of assurance. The enemy will have nothing on you!

How beautiful you are! How radiant! Storms uncover things, and what they are doing is uncovering and revealing not only to you but to others, the strength, and stamina I've placed in you. It's not about getting everything right, but it's simply about standing in the midst, remaining and being unmoved. The great thing about storms, though, is that they do pass.

About Emotions

Entry #210

Emotions are beautiful and good when they are led by your spirit man. In the leading of My Spirit you must comply. Remember to take every thought captive and let the fear of man fall to the wayside. It has nothing on you and Me. This is what I will share with you. I created your emotions, but I also gave you a will. Emotions can be like a misguided missile if they are not submitted to Me. They can spin off and cause things to happen apart from My intentions.

Submit every part of your being to Me. Meekness is the ability to control the power of your emotions. Ask Me for it. Now I am not asking you to abstain from joy and laughter. Hardly! You would be abstaining from My nature if you did that! I believe you know that I am referring to trusting you with how to handle things. There is a discipline to be had, but I am a good Father, training you in the ways you should go. Celebrate your emotions, be thankful for them; but at the same time submit them to Me, and I will teach you how to handle them. I love you and I adore the way I've made you.

Advancement Is a Choice

Entry #211

I want to advance you to the next level, a greater level of focus and awareness. It will require self-discipline and self-control. These are already in you; just pull them up and choose them with your will. Have you not been asking Me for a greater focus and awareness? I want you to know I've heard you and I'm answering you.

Your will is a powerful thing. It is what I am working with. I must be able to trust you with greater responsibilities. To do this, I must know that your will is submitted to Me above yourself. As you advance, it can be dangerous for you to step out on your own apart from My leading. Think of it like a military rank. You must trust your leader. What happens when you step out on your own? You have broken rank. You've let your will override My wisdom. Keep yourself in check and trust My leadership. It is for your own protection. Remember, I am all-knowing and wise. It's just a matter of setting the old pride and ego aside. Yes, awareness is coming to you. I am sending it to you in increments. I am going to make you unafraid of man.

You have been gifted with many talents. You are a natural leader, but apart from My training, you would be like a wild stallion. A wild stallion is beautiful to look at, but what good is it unless it is broken in for a greater purpose. A free spirit is only bliss for a short time; it is short lived. Wisdom and dedication are a better choice; not to lose your childlike wonder, but to submit yourself to the One who can draw out your full potential. Wisdom chooses wisely. The choice is yours.

An Introduction to Your Music Class

Entry #212

I want you to be able to hear Me clearly in any setting and this requires a discipline. Disciplines start off like little seedlings. I will help you pay attention to them and will take time nurturing them, removing the weeds so the seeds can grow properly. While you learn these new disciplines, your flesh may get a bit anxious and trigger your emotions to well up out of control. Emotions are beautiful when they are submitted to Me. They can then operate the way they were designed to be. Let Me guide these powerful expressions of yours. They are the colors and sounds of your personality. If you'll entrust them to Me, I can add depth and structure to these hues and sounds.

Unruly emotions can be like an amateur musician. When given the music to play, notes go flying all over the place! The amateur musician has not taken the time to practice. He only wanted to play. He may be passionate and zealous, but there is no trace of the song he attempts to play. No one can follow or enjoy its melody.

I would like to train you to listen and become an excellent musician. The best musicians have learned the art of managing the highs and lows of the song and of playing out the emotion like a beautiful dancing silhouette. They can capture the moments and gently release them, for they have learned the discipline of where to increase and decrease the sound.

Yield to the Master Conductor, yours truly, Holy Spirit. Have a watchful eye and a listening ear. Practice engaging with and responding to His cues. No one knows music like He does, and no one knows emotions like He does. Take your cues from Him. Follow His leadings and promptings. He knows the perfect timing of the music, the rest notes, the crescendos, and the decrescendos. Everything there is to know is within His musical knowledge! It is this way in your life. He can show you how to live in sync, in melody, and in rhythm with Him. So, yield your beautiful sounds and colors to Him, the Master Conductor, and He will draw out of you the most amazing composition!

Limitless Freedom

Entry #213

Freedom... Isn't it what your heart longs for? Do you think mankind was ever created to live in a box? Boxes are manmade, and man chooses to adapt to them. Limiting and confining, they stunt the growth and possibilities of man. I am limitless and filled with endless possibilities, and that is how I've designed you to be. Was it not I who made you in My image and likeness? Then why are you choosing to limit yourself? I want you to challenge yourself to break the limits that you or man has placed on you. Break down and break through the boxes of mindsets and confinements. It's time to expand and stretch your wings.

Do you want to see and experience what I've really placed in you? You're a masterpiece, destined to "ooh and ahh" the multitudes. This is for My glory, and oh what a joy it will be for you as you expand and take leaps of faith. Freedom is found in the leaps of faith! It's just as much of a risk not to change as it is to change. Take the risk. Is a life of regret worth it?

I am your assurance. It's time to grow again and go farther than you've ever gone before. Tag... you're it! Start running! Your destiny is egging you on! Set yourself free and thrive with Me! I hold the keys and I'm handing them to you for your freedom and your destiny!

The Puzzle Piece Called Choice

Entry #214

Walk as My sons and daughters, no longer as peasants. You must take on the identity I've called you to. I became poor for you, not so that you could remain poor. Cast off the old you. It no longer exists. My gravestone was your gravestone. My resurrection is now your resurrection. Your life is now found in your new identity in Me. Know who you are! Stand in who you are!

Let Me train you, prove you, and supply you with all you will need. You make the choice with your will. You can either choose to be a peasant or adopt your new nature and rule and reign with Me. You are princes and princesses in My kingdom! This is your true DNA. The only thing missing is your choosing it, so put your missing piece in place and watch the full picture unfold. Ask My Holy Spirit to accompany you. He will tutor you in My royal ways. He'll teach you how to dress, how to walk, how to think, and how to talk. He holds all the keys and resources you need. Enroll in My royal training course. Agree to your new identity. I have chosen you and you have chosen Me.

Understanding the Power of Your Will

Entry #215

Before I created the earth, there was darkness. What I had envisioned was still inside Me, but what happened when I spoke the words? It became what I spoke. I have given you the same ability. Take it not lightly, for you are My offspring and I desire for you to create as I create. Much is going to be entrusted to you as you step out and start using the gift I've given you. Yes, an increase is on its way. What would you like to create with Me? Speak it out. It is not that hard. Don't worry about your faith. Speak it out and keep speaking it out, and your faith will catch up with you. This is a matter of being willing. Your will is more powerful than you know! Why do you think the enemy wants to break your will? He wants to stop you from standing in My image, declaring and responding like I do. He wants to either break your will to stop you from creating or give you a bad taste in life so you'll produce a negative effect with your mouth; so he either wants to break it or curve it. Don't let him! WILL to not let him! Your will is powerful and a force to be reckoned with!

I want you to ask Me more about how I want you to use your will. Let Me train you and teach you. Take ownership of its power and stand in who you are! With your will, tell the enemy to loose everything that belongs to you! With your will, receive My abundant grace for your life. Start willing to do everything I've asked you to and you'll watch yourself fall into line and in sync with that action. Will. Make your mind up and do it! Speak it, create it, and model it!

Patient Pursuit

Entry #216

I know this is new ground for you. I've asked you to set your hands to the ideas I've given you and now you are in motion with it. Be sure not to give up or give in too soon. Seeds don't sprout the moment you plant them, but the germination process begins. A baby isn't born the moment it's conceived, but it begins its development in that moment. Patience is all that is needed and the pursuit of preparation with expectation.

Picture it like this... I've asked you to go fishing. As we speak, I am lining up the fish by your act of obedience. Now how would you catch the fish, if you didn't first get into a boat? The gifts I've given you are the bait. It is My anointing that will lure them. Now would you catch any fish, if you didn't drop the line? Of course, not. Next comes the patient pursuit of trolling the waters, seeking and finding…but remember who brings the fish. The fish are there in the water as you engage. Are you beginning to see that with Me everything is an opportunity for relational teamwork? This is how you learn and this is how you grow. Remember, I am your Papa, not just your God. I want to teach you how My kingdom business works. This takes both of us engaging together and both of us being intentional.

Are You Ready for the Ride of a Lifetime?

Entry #217

Because of where I am taking you spiritually, I have increased your level of praying in the Spirit. It is equipping you to go deeper. There's no way around it; it is your next task and upgrade in the road. Think of it like getting on a horse. You've been used to going by foot, but you can only go so fast. I am accelerating things in you now, so it's time to get on the horse and stay on the horse! Let My Spirit do the work! Draw deep into Me and I will take you where you need to go. Are you ready for the ride of a lifetime?

There is a rhythm in riding a horse. You have to be in sync. I am teaching and training you how to be in rhythm and in sync with Me. Let us become so one! This is what I desire for you.

Let me give you My thoughts. Listen to My whisper. A rider rides a horse through promptings and leadings. A horse moves as one with its rider through its willingness to yield. You have a heart that is willing to yield and that is why I have chosen you. Endurance is needed, but I've already been conditioning you. Are you ready to move with Me, train with Me, and develop new inner muscles? I believe that you are and that is why I have invited you into this.

Prepare for Take-off!
10...9...8...7...6...

Entry #218

You are like an astronaut being buckled in. I have prepared you and am buckling you in for the ride of your life! I am preparing to launch you. Stop all the fuss (LOL)! I am doing all the double checks. Just rest in your seat and wait for me to initiate. The countdown is beginning to take place!

Your Patience Course is almost done. Don't take this waiting process so personally. I have had to prepare places and people for you, so don't think this waiting is all because of what you are doing or not doing right. It's about timing and positioning. Be patient and trust Me. Enjoy the rest of this cycle, knowing that I'm aligning everything.

Keep surrendering your viewpoints. Everything will work out as planned. Trust Me, trust Me, trust Me. Keep "eating" out of My hand and you will not miss a thing for sure! Allow Me to sensitize you and put you completely at rest, pliable in My hands. Chuck fear out the window and embrace My grace and love!

Calculated Risks

Entry #219

A calculated risk is stepping out in faith to a place of direction and utterance from Me. It's not stepping out blindly without My release or permission. I will give you the confidence and make it smooth. I will put your heart at ease.

Let go of every hindrance no matter what it feels like. I need your full attention. You are not your circumstances. Embrace the invisible rope of grace and climb up into My lap!

I am proud of you for taking the risks I've asked you to take. I know they don't always make sense to the human mind, but that's OK. All I'm asking for is your obedience. It will make sense afterward, for I will have upgraded your perspective. This is a grand plan I have for you! Take the risks at My leading and discover the great oasis of freedom I've destined for you! There are mysteries to be uncovered and gems to be discovered! Take the risk with Me and safe you shall be!

You're My Voice in the Earth

Entry #220

Open your mouth and I will fill it! A greater anointing is coming your way. You've been passing the tests and I am pleased. Passing doesn't mean you get everything right, but overall you are advancing. You are right on track! I have disciplined your mouth to submit to Me. Again, this doesn't mean getting everything right or perfect. It's a process, but you are a willing vessel. Through you I will release many, many decrees.
I am raising you up to be a voice in the earth! A voice that sounds the alarm, heralds My announcements, and establishes My ways. This is no small thing and no small task. That is why this journey has been creating in you a bend, bending you to lean completely on Me.

Before this, you relied on your own good nature and strength. You wanted to do something great for Me! And oh, yes, you will and are. But back then it would have been a cause for your ego to preside and take the lead instead of Me. I have done such a work in you! Now, you truly only harken to your Shepherd's voice.

I know your love for Me runs deep! I have invested and sought out much in you. You will truly say, "If not for the Lord I would not be standing". Once you gloried in your strength; now you have taken the high road which is the low road, and have found that there is much more glory in weakness. It is a brilliant oxymoron, don't you think, for you are valued higher in your weakened state from My point of view. True humility has bloomed forth and is now releasing the intoxicating fragrance of Me and My Kingdom. My nature is pouring forth from you. Your trials have stained you in the color of My blood for grace has triumphed over all. Your surrender is as fine gold to Me. Oh, can you see what I've brought forth in you? Nothing was lost!

Your voice has been transformed! It now heralds with the display and frequencies of heaven! My sheep shall hear your voice and come running in for they can see My permanent residence in you! When they hear you speak, they hear Me. Thank you for saying yes to My process, yes to the journey, and yes to My heart. I love you!

Adapting to the Passenger Seat

Entry #221

Allow the process to take place and form you. There are precious things that emerge from the pressure, hard places, heat, and irritations, such as natural diamonds, gold and pearls. The work I am doing in you will be like this, but what emerges will far outweigh their value! Yes, there is a cost...but there is a rarity in those who are willing to go all the way. It will be worth it!

Letting go is one of the biggest keys to making it through the process. Your flesh will fight to be right and look for the closest exit. It's uncomfortable being "out of control," but you really only have two choices--to be in "your" control or to be in "My" control. We can't be having two drivers at the wheel. That would be quite a hairy ride, don't you think...fighting over the wheel? Part of this journey is about getting used to and comfortable with being in the passenger seat, casting your cares on Me, and enjoying the beauty of the scenery.

Now you're not being irresponsible because you're still hanging with Me. You're just yielding your ways of doing things to My way of doing things. There's only one vehicle. You're just choosing daily to let Me be Lord of your life in every situation, emotion, and circumstance. Recognize that I am your covering and you are now living in Me. I am responsible for you. Just keep yielding to the journey I am taking you on. If it gets too overwhelming at times, sit back and close your eyes. Sink back into My faithfulness and simply meditate on who I am. You'll once again feel secure enough to let Me drive. The farther we go like this, the greater your value will increase. The heat of this kind of inner discipline is making you rich without your even realizing it.

Your Victory Is Just a Belief Away

Entry #222

Your victory is just a belief away! Listen! The money to do the things you desire is coming. I desire for you to take steps of faith in the direction I have been showing you. I will make My timing perfect for you. You don't have to fear that it will be ahead of time or out of step. Just keep yielding in your relationship with Me.

Stay out of fear and remain in rest. Yes, many things are coming down the line, but know this; you will also be able to handle it well. This is your race, no one else's; so don't compare, just obey with a cheerful heart. You will not sink. In fact, you will flourish!

I'm placing My hands on the side of your eyes like blinders to keep you from looking at anything else or anyone else but Me. This takes a yielding and a discipline, but you are going to find quite the enjoyment in it. These "blinders" by your eyes will also affect your heart to keep it in line with seeing things My way. You can rest in what you know about Me, not so much in what you see. Let your heart do the reassuring. Trust resides at the residence of your belief. Are you ready to trust Me all the way? The more you do, the more victory opens to you. Sit back and simply agree with what I said I've already done for you. That's right, you've got it!

Investment and Harvest

Entry #223

I am coming to invest but also to harvest from the gifts I've placed in you. The fruit is beginning to take form and color for I have been ripening you. I have plans to harvest you, so cultivate! Cultivate with Me. I've given you everything you need. You don't need all the pieces up front, just the one for the next step. Take it, for the fruit is appearing!

Plant all that I have given you. I have storehouses in mind and their mouths will open to receive you. Work diligently as I lead you. It's time for you to work in My gardens. Set your mind on the things of the Kingdom, the things I've asked you to do, and I will take care of the rest.

I reward those who diligently seek Me, believe Me, and act upon My words. You will profit much! Watch and get ready! You are going to be overwhelmed in a great way at the harvest I will bring through you. Stay steady, but also rest when I lead you to. I am going to teach you how to live in a healthy balance. There is no burnout in My Kingdom. The things I ask you to do will refuel you because you are designed for what I'm asking of you. It will be the right fuel in the right car. We are in this together! You are going to have a blast doing this with Me! Keep listening, stilling yourself and writing down the plans of what I want next. We make a great team, don't you think? You're doing a good job and I am proud of you! I know I'm stretching you, but trust Me. You're going to love the results!

Come In and Dine with Me

Entry #224

Dining in My presence is quite satisfying, for I am a fine drink for all who thirst. The meals I prepare are of the highest quality. Is your soul thirsty? Then come to Me. Let me refuel you. Let Me re-nourish you. Health and life are only found in Me. Do you need to seek clarity? Come to My table.

Let's converse. What is it you're asking? What would you like to know? My door is always open to you and I have a seat with your name on it. So, come, let's meet at My table. What would you like? What will satisfy you? Are you looking for meat? Do you desire something sweet? Are you hungry for revelation or even for a friendship? I can be all of these to you, if you'll enter in. I long for and await the presence of your company, just as you long for and await Mine. So, shall we join and meet then? Allow yourself to go there... no more distractions or excuses. Cut off the pulls that keep you from Me. Arouse your desire and expect to be delighted. No obligation, only comfort and rest. I am your safe place.

Allow Me to minister to your soul and comfort you. Allow Me to reassure you and instruct you. I love being your Father! I miss our times together! Oh, won't you come and simply be with Me again? No strings attached... no work, no labor. Just be, just simply be with Me. That's what I desire, Beloved. Does this sound too good to be true? That's what the world would say. But you and I both know it's true. You've experienced Me many times like this before. Come! Come away with Me and receive from My vine of eternity. I am your supply and I am your source. Shake off and dance off the cares of this world. Rest your head upon My heart and listen as I whisper in your ear wisdom's answers to your prayers. I delight in you. Oh! I delight in you. Will you give Me time? Will you come and dine? What is it you desire? I will set the table and prepare it for you! Come My sweet one, My cherished one. I long for your presence and you long for Mine.

Slam the Door on the Enemy's Fingers

Entry #225

Your doubts are coming from fear... and where does this fear come from? "Pain?" Yes, at times; but let me suggest to you even more so where these fears and doubts are coming from. They are strategic darts from the enemy to convince you, in your emotions, to believe something that's untrue about yourself and the circumstance you're in. Yes, your emotions are a gateway. That's why you must stand guard and capture every thought that tries to come through your door. The easiest way to deal with this is to slam the door on the enemy's fingers for even thinking he could cross over your threshold and enter in. Kick him out and close the door on him! He will be forced to feel the effects and see the sign of truth posted on it, for My spirit lives within you and has taken up residence. He has placed His door of truth at the gateways of your soul! This is your protection and it's always available to you! All I need from you is your willingness to choose to slam the door in the enemy's face! You can do it every time he approaches at your doorstep with lying, fiery darts!

Come into agreement with Me no matter how you feel or what you see. Pay no attention to the past for it has no ties to today. My mercies are with you and every new day is a gift to you. You are free to hit the reset button every day! That is how much grace is offered to you! I have more than enough to pour over you!

You're getting stronger and stronger, but do you know what's even better than that? You're getting stronger and stronger at being dependent on Me! That's what the enemy's afraid of! He knows he's no match for Me, and he's no match for you once you realize who you are! I love you and I'm proud of your journey! You're growing leaps and bounds! Shake the dust of the past off your feet. Dive into My refreshing stream and watch the enemy scream!! Victory is yours, dear one!

My Promise and Commitment to You

Entry #226

You have dedicated your life to Me and have shared your commitment to Me. And now, let Me share Mine with you. I promise to tend to your needs like a good shepherd would. I promise to always be mindful of your desires and likes. I promise to shield you from the enemy's attacks and always guide you into safety. I am your shield and defense. You can trust Me. I promise to give you a heavenly perspective and not an earthly one. I promise to reveal My heart to you. I promise to empower you. I promise to always keep you out of harm's way. My protection will forever surround you. I promise to provide for you financially. I promise to heal your soul. I promise to make you so happy that you'll choose my life easily over yours. I promise not to leave you suffering. I promise to equip you and strengthen you. I promise to love you with My unconditional love and cherish you like no other. I promise to surround you with My angelic host, who will always be ready at your disposal for whatever you need. I promise to listen to your heart and be tender with you. I know what you can handle. I promise to let you hear My voice clearly.

I am so pleased that you have made the decision and commitment to follow Me, and I'm pleased to offer mine to you. You won't be disappointed! I love you and am committed to you! You can trust Me in this and rest upon My words.

The Awakening Has Begun

Entry #227

Get ready to see an awakening...I want unity in My church as well as in the workplace. There should be no separation within the mindset of My people. My bride is not a split personality. I want her to resemble Me whether she is in the workplace or in the church building gathering with family. Soon the world will witness that the true bride has arisen as the church! The old labels will begin to fall off and people will re-invest in My church once again, because they are going to taste and see the true, the real, and the genuine.

The world is waiting to see Me and find Me in My people called the church. They want to believe, but they have not fully seen nor felt My image displayed. It has been fragmented and a bit confusing to the onlookers, but no more! I am arising in My bride and they are going to see Me fully this time! It's the time for fullness and you are a key player in resembling and leading this by your nature, attitude, belief, and ability. You will be a sign and witness pointing them to the truth they've been looking for.

Everyone in the earth knows there is a power beyond themselves. They want to understand where they've originated from. I have turned the key and I am pouring out the clear revelation they need. I now have a body in the earth that is willing to represent Me without tainted motives. Their heart is to share family life and invite all those in who desire the same. Oh, what glorious days await you!! It is time to engage and be who I've fully designed you to be!! This is the age of fullness and demonstration in the earth!

Stay Diligent and Trust Me

Entry #228

I completely understand what you are going through, but the pillars I am placing in you are stronger than steel! Be about My purposes. They look like everything I've been showing you and what you know to be true in your heart. Take it serious! You must prepare, just like you would if you were traveling or even more so if a baby was being born. Preparation is a must.

Pride no longer has a hold on you, for I have removed it and replaced it with a humble heart. This is so that you can carry the mantles and gifts I desire to release through you! Thank you for allowing Me to make you a ready vessel, one who is truly devoted to me with your time and energy. I will use you in ways you never thought possible! I am answering the prayers of those who prayed for you in the early days of your life. They will be amazed and witness that I truly have not forgotten their prayers. Many have plowed the field ahead of you. They have paid their "dues" so you could thrive! You are carrying a harvest within you! They are cheering you on from heaven and on the earth. Your life has been ordained for this time! There is more in you than you realize!! Watch and be amazed!

You have been through the death process and now the seed is cracking forth with new life, for my breath and purposes have germinated your seed, and oh, what a harvest you will bring! Stay diligent and trust Me! I am truly ordering your steps and placing you in the fields that you're called to plant in and influence. Keep a trusting and restful heart in Me. I am going to make you more sensitive than ever to My leading and promptings! You won't miss it! The days are bright and your harvest will be ripe! All of heaven is cheering you on!

Illusions

Entry #229

Try not to guess at My ways of operation. Those belong to Me alone. When you guess at it, you replace trust. I would rather you trust Me and be surprised by My amazing ways of doing things. I bet you'll never figure it out, and that's the point! I won't let you figure it out. Why? Because I want you to be led by Me. I want you to be secure in My choices, even when they don't make sense.

So, what's your part? Simply to come to Me. I will either make you aware of what I'm up to, or I will comfort and support you in taking the leap of faith even when you can't see. This is supposed to be an adventure of discovery. You are discovering how to live in Me, flow with Me, and give up all control and reasoning.

I share this to encourage you. If you control, you limit yourself. Do you really want to limit yourself? Or would you like to explore just how amazing I can be in your life? Taking the leap is like exercising a muscle. It takes a bit of development, but the more you do it the stronger you will feel. Right now, it feels impossible and looks impossible, but that's the before. Once you take the leap and cross the other side, what shifts? The realization that it is now possible.

Illusions are so deceitful. They keep My people hindered way too much. It is a simple change of belief' followed through by action, that breaks through an illusion. Truth is the driving force. That is why more than ever My people need to refresh themselves with My truth. If you want to erase the illusions, flood yourself with truth and let it spill over into complete action! Good results are sure to follow and the impossible soon becomes possible.

Faith to Step Out

Entry #230

Go where I send you. Your obedience will be rewarded. Go where I send you, for there is a higher purpose than you can see. As you engage with My instructions, more doors will begin to open. They will remain shut until you take steps towards them. My favor will go with you. You don't have to be afraid of missing it. No, not at all. For you are not alone; I am with you! I am a good father and I will make sure you have everything you need to succeed at this, only move forward in faith.

Not everything will be picture-perfect clear. If that was the case, then there would be no need for faith, there would be no need for Me. Many of My children pray and ask Me for clarity. But what they are often saying by that request is that they are too afraid to take the risk, too afraid to listen to My still small voice. They want all the puzzle pieces first before they make the leap, when I am only offering the next piece. Don't you think it's better that I hold the puzzle pieces for you? I am a master at the timing of things. That is why you must entrust Me with the whole picture!

I so want to do life with you! Be not afraid to do life with Me. I know you want answers. I know you are cautious to step out; but I guarantee you, the more time you spend with Me the more confident you will be.

You and I are like three-legged race partners trying to get our rhythm down! You want to go one way and I'm saying to go another. You sometimes want to go fast, and I'm saying slow down or vice versa. But you know what? We're getting better together. You're going to be amazed at how in sync we're going to become with each other. I'm not concerned with the process. All I need is a willing heart to work with and I know you always are. I don't listen to your fleshly outbursts! I listen to your heart. Listen, I am faithful and I know you're aware of that. You are aware and you do believe, but I want you to experience My faithfulness even more. There is something experience does to a human being that can't be taken away. Head knowledge is often forgotten, but experiences hardly ever fade. You and I are experiencing life together. You are learning how to walk with Me. Yes! We're tied together in a good way, linked arm in arm, discovering and experiencing who I am and who you are with each step! I love you and am willing to walk this entire journey out with you. You are going to continue to experience Me and never be the same!

Today

Entry #231

If you turn the page ahead of time, you miss key parts of a story. Did you know that today is a key part? Never underestimate paying attention to and living in the now. NOW is what I want to give you. So, let's explore the now. I really want you to value today, looking for Me in today. If you skip this page, you'll miss the treasures I have hidden for you to discover today. If I created today, why would you want to look past it? Is there not value in today? Why is one day more important than the other? Are they not all equally important? Yes, some days carry the weightier things, but it takes living in today to get to those tomorrows. It took living in the todays to build the tomorrows. Can you imagine having a cake that was made without using all the ingredients? I want you to look at today like another ingredient. Discover and gather the ingredients that are present today.

I do not measure value the way you do, in sizes of greatness and such. Mankind thinks the bigger the package the better the gift. Well, last time I checked, diamonds came in small packages. I value greatness in each of the many building blocks, not one left behind or taken for granted. Don't look at the grandness of an event that is "sure" to change your life in the future. Yes, it will bring some change but not without the value of micro changes in a daily walk with Me. Micros are more powerful than the "grand." Micros are what shape you. Allow today to shape you and mold you. Allow yourself to rest on My potter's wheel today. The finished product will come, but not without the daily allowance and touch of my hand. Everything is fashioned and formed. Embrace My blessings and embrace My fashioning of you today. Every day is necessary. Each day is a gift.

The Mark of Peace

Entry #232

My peace surpasses all understanding. This will be My mark upon you. People will not understand it, but they'll know they want it. You are a carrier of heaven's atmosphere, whether you realize it or not. Sometimes you are so used to it that you don't realize how strong and contrasting it is to the crowd around you. Let them taste, see, and experience Me in you. You've been marked by My greatness and display My personality. People will know that you come from Me.

I am about ready to give you language to describe the heavenly things. I want My people to know how real I am and just how much I am involved with everything they experience; told and untold. The supernatural is now becoming more real and tangible than ever before and I want you to be one of My representatives in it.

Stay very close to Me in these assignments of life. I need you to be close, like a rider and his trusted steed, so to speak. The horse and rider are so close the communication comes through the promptings of touch, like an inner touch from the rider to the horse. Great sensitivity is being added to you. Keep hungering for it and I will continue to fill you!

In Between the Sets of Waves

Entry #233

Now, Sweetheart, you know I'm not going to tell you all the answers. I want you to trust Me and follow. Just keep preparing during this lull between the sets of waves. You must tread water, so you're still being productive and staying above the water. Keep rising to the occasion where you are right now, and allow me to send you and guide you to the right waves to pick you up. You can't always see when a wave comes. That's why they are called sneaker waves. You must allow time for it to be positioned. Allow Me to be strategic in your life. Just keep treading the water. I will bring the wave soon.

What are the benefits of treading water? Well, let's look at it in spiritual terms. I am toning and disciplining your inner-man. But to do this, you must remain in the water. Yes, this requires more endurance, but you can only catch the waves if you're already in the water. I know you have your eyes wide open and you're just waiting for the cue. Trust Me, I know you're ready. But what you need more than anything is continued patience. This is what makes the best wave riders - ones that don't want to jump out ahead of Me, but are stilling their will to take the immediate risk when I compel them. So, Sweet One, let patience have its perfect work in you. You're not missing it. Just trust that I am aligning things and live from an eternal standpoint where there are no time frames.

Obedience trumps any act done apart from My direction. Many men do things in their own strength, but you are learning the steady endurance of staying power in the wait. How do you think you could be taking care of what you're doing right now, if you were busy riding the wave? Give equal value to both the wave and the wait in between; each is important. Trust Me. You'll thank Me for this advice.
You're doing well though. Keep it up! For

soon and unbeknownst to you, the wave will suddenly be approaching and lift you up onto it.

Combating Fear and Frustration

Entry #234

Don't you know that you're right on track? Am I that insensitive and fickle that you'd feel ashamed, if you were off track in the slightest way? Sweetheart, I'm bigger than that. You're putting too much emphasis and confidence in your own abilities. Who's the one who found you and saved you? Let's try putting some of that confidence back on Me. Release yourself, let go of yourself, and put your hands back in the hand hold of grace.

You're frustrated because you know you can't do anything about your situation right now. Did you ever think that's right where I want you to be? I want you to realize your incompleteness without Me.

Conclude that you need Me; be OK with it and rest in it. Society labels this as weakness, and that's why you're struggling with the idea. But in My Kingdom, it's greatness, because you are truly acknowledging My lordship, ability, and salvation. What honorable king doesn't want to be depended on? I am breaking the independence off your soul, if you really want to know what's going on.

Practice trusting instead of fearing. Make the exchange. If you're afraid of getting hurt, shouldn't you be more afraid of the damaging effects of fear instead of faith? Yes, disappointment is painful, but fear will lead you to more disappointment by far. If you could only see the benefits faith brings to your body, you'd trust Me more. Fear robs you, self-effort suppresses you, and nothing negative will ever benefit you; so why entertain its thoughts and submit to its grip? You think you're in control, but it's controlling you.

Open the floodgates of truth, My truth, and let it pour out violently against all these debilitating thoughts! Believe Me,

My truth will win out! Now go, combat the lies and fill yourself with My word. This action alone will replace the reactions you've been feeling.

A Good Dose of Meditation

Entry #235

I want you to meditate on My greatness and bigness in your life. You see your abilities as bigger than Mine sometimes. What's that about? Do you think you might be battling with some trust issues? How do you think we can find resolve in that? Do you know that My truth will always lead you to victory?
In society people are self-medicating daily just to make it through, but what they may need is a good dose of meditation.

That's why many in the Bible said to meditate daily. Meditate on My truths. Think of it like this, you can't eat just once and expect to live. You must eat certain things every day to get the nutrition and benefits your body needs. So, it is with

My word. Take your daily doses. It's important to your spiritual health. You know how they say certain foods are brain food. Well, My word is heart food. If you're feeling empty, fill up on it. It's good for the soul! Not only will it fill the void, but it will satisfy and nourish your hunger too. It's a simple fix. Pills only last so long. They're temporary fixes.

The reality is, if you're hungry, by all means eat! No more denying yourself or making excuses. My food will heal and satisfy you with no setbacks or side effects. The only way you're going to get the results you want in any area is by taking the necessary action. That's it. It really is that simple. Chuck the counterfeits and grab hold of the things that will nourish you and last.

The Beauty Aid

Entry #236

You don't have to worry about your future. The new you is in an eternal state, so I don't want you focusing on your age anymore. You're renewed with My eternal life stream flowing through you. You've been looking for the fountain of youth all your life, but do you not know that I'm the drink you've been looking for? Drink of Me like never before, and I will renew your youth daily. People will begin to say to you things like: "Your countenance is changing!" "You look younger!" "What are you doing?" "What are you taking?" You're drinking the drink called "The River of Life." You're taking the pill called "The Pill of Christ." I am becoming one with you. When you consume me, like a beauty aid, the results are fantastic! You are what you eat. I know you know that.

You are My bride and My delight. Do you know I delight in you? I'm not after or looking at any of your flaws. Love sees no flaws. I see My beautiful one, the one I brought forth. You have My DNA and I am honored by you. I know you may not always believe this, but it's true. You are beautiful and I want you to receive it and choose to believe it. If you believe it, life will emanate out of you in the most beautiful way. This is not prideful; it's an act of thankfulness and appreciation, thanking your Creator and Dad. I love you! There's no one quite like you and I made you that way on purpose. So, start celebrating even more so the wonderful form and creation I've made you. You are smart! You are smart! Oh, if you only knew what I have in store for you! I'm about to surprise you again! Keep running, walking, and talking with Me. We are in this life together. I want to bless you, and I want you to receive it. We're about to have a lot of fun together. Live a surrendered life. The joy, happiness, and energy you're longing for are going to start flooding into your life as you let go and lean on Me. It's that happy spot in life.

Take Flight for New Sight

Entry #237

Keep your wings strong. Here's what "wings" can do in a spiritual sense. They can raise your perceptions and perspectives; they are like lenses to see who I am and how to take life when it comes at you. You can allow your wings to lift you up or take you down by what you believe. Wings follow what the heart and brain tells them. The power of belief will lift you up or keep you grounded.

So, let's look at this in a physical sense--a little history on airplane wings. In the physical, the wings must be greater in span than the weight of the plane to get lift. So, let's say the body of your plane represents the weight of the circumstances you're carrying in life right now. Your goal is to enhance your wing span to be greater than the weight by taking the perspective of the situation to a higher and greater altitude!

Do you know that things that live on the ground level pass out if you take them to a high altitude? Your Spirit was made to soar at high levels with Me! What I want is for all the negative thoughts and destructive critters to pass out. They can't last in the altitudes of My perspectives; this is a key in My Kingdom. The enemy wants to keep you bogged down, tied down, and limited. He does his best work at ground level thinking. He wants to cast a storm above you in the stirring of your imagination to keep you from taking flight! You must align yourself with the runway, hit the accelerator, and pull up! The key is to relocate your perceptions, perspectives, and lenses to a higher altitude. You'll see a lot more clearly. Your sight is limited on the ground; I want you high in the sky with Me. I am going to teach you how to look at things differently. Your life flow and spiritual oxygen are up high, so get off the ground. Take advantage of the force of your circumstances. Allow the force to thrust you upward! Stretch out your wings wide and broad and come up with Me. Everything is useful for advancement in My kingdom.

You Will Make It!

Entry #238

You will make it! I give you My word. Just keep your wings steady... or keep your emotions stabilized. This is My promise to you--whatever you have had to give up in this journey I will give back to you ten times more! Nothing is lost in My Kingdom. I keep track of everything and I have been keeping track of you. Rejoice in the goodness you know about Me. Let patience lift you up and keep you afloat. By doing this, you'll outlast the enemy.

Remain childlike and rely on My grace and mercy. Surely I am not a hard God. If earthly fathers are willing to help their children, how much more am I? Deeper things are taking place than you can see right now. Continue to let go and flow with Me. I will orchestrate things accordingly.

Safeguard Your Decisions

Entry #239

You must learn to kick Reason and Logic to the wayside. Do not listen to them. They want to be their own god and use you to do it! These are the names of two lying spirits that try to influence your mind and deceive your decision-making, convincing you that these thoughts are your ideas. They want you to override what I have shared with you to do. They stroke your ego to cause you to pull back and believe you're choosing the "right path" by protecting yourself, when in reality you've been duped by two little lying spirits.

These two always appear when you are deciding to follow My ways outside of what seems "normal." They convince you that you must stay with what's familiar, and then in comes the third spirit, Familiarity. This third spirit convinces you it's safe to stay in the familiar. Watch out for these three when I'm asking you to change course or enter something new. If their words are in opposition with what I've shared with you, then allow My truth to expose them for who they really are, your enemy.

My ways may not always make sense. That's where faith and trust come in. Know My voice and My ways better than anything else in life and you won't be sidetracked, derailed or "miss-lead" by the deceiving voices of Reason, Logic, and Familiarity.

Your Heavenly Language and Spiritual Growth

Entry #240

Many of My people are brokenhearted because they have not understood My ways. They were trying to discern Me through their minds, while all this time they had underdeveloped spirits. Pray much in the spirit and you shall hear Me more clearly and you shall see more brightly.

Many are walking around with dim lights (spiritual insight) not knowing where or how to make it brighter. You must stir up your spirit like a turbine that produces energy. What's true in the natural is oftentimes true in the spirit. My word says to stir yourself up. The same was true in the old days when they used to pedal a bike to produce electricity. If you'd like "electricity" to power things up in your spiritual life, pray in the spirit! If you don't know how, then ask Me to baptize you and fill you up with My Spirit! A new language shall well up from your innermost being for it is the language of heaven--as in heaven so on earth. Would you like My language? I speak yours, now how about receiving mine? All you have to do is simply ask, believe, receive, and start thanking and praising Me. It will come in a seed form. I will water and breathe upon it and it will come bursting forth.

If you would like more understanding about praying in the spirit, search My Word and ask close friends who you believe share this same language of heaven. It is free and I am offering it to you. If you would like power to operate in Kingdom things, receive the gift of My Spirit and begin to speak the language. Now you may not understand what's being said, but how is that any different from understanding another country's language? Yet don't the words of another country have just as much power and meaning as yours? So, think it not strange, this heavenly language you are about to receive, for truly it is natural to your spirit.

You're very being came from Me! Praying in the spirit helps remove debris so you can see and hear clearly. Rest, allow, and flow with the live stream frequencies coming from heaven! Declarations are pronounced when you pray in this language. Power is released, angels are commissioned, and prayers are being answered. The truth is being spoken and spiritual growth is being added to you, along with wisdom, counsel, revelation, and understanding. All the benefits of heaven are accessible to you. Pray much in the spirit and all this will come flooding into your life like a life-giving river, bringing life to all the seeds I've planted inside you! Great things take place when you pray in the spirit! Enjoy this new heavenly language for it comes from the place that you originated from.

Depression

Entry #241

Depression is always linked to self-effort. It hooks itself into the underlying bedrock of pride. It crouches and waits for its next victim's failure, piling on more rocks of guilt and shame to keep him held under and weighed down by self-inflicting judgments, blurring his vision by boulders of indecision. Only in us (Father, Son, & Holy Spirit) can one be set free! If My people will obey Me, then they will see. If My people will obey Me, then they will hear. If My people will obey Me, then they shall walk freely and lightly for My ways are easy; so easy a little child could understand them. That is why many miss it. It is too simple. Man, wants something to achieve, to be commended for. All this leads to is a downward spiral of uncertainty, mishandling, and failure down the road of independence. Isn't that how we all got here in the first place; mankind took the roadway of independence?

If you long for true life free from fear, free from depression, and free from the cares of this world... become one with Me. Take on a new name and a new way of doing things. I am Christ. I came so that you would have life and that more abundantly. All who enter in through Me live a life of peace and surrender. They handle and view life from a completely different perspective. They no longer live under their circumstances with all the turmoil they bring. They live from a viewpoint above their circumstances by taking on My eyesight. I help them see the hidden seeds of prosperity, the diamonds in the rough, and the gold hidden in the darkness. When you live with Me life becomes a treasure hunt.

You can either live with Me or continue going at life in your own strength, battling the boulders of depression. Come to Me and I will give you rest. Come to Me and I will give you the drink of life that will last. If you are thirsty, I am the one you've been longing for. Feed no more upon your troubles. Set your gaze on Me, fill yourself up on Me, and you shall be satisfied. I will bring you up higher and teach you My ways. Simply turn from what you've been doing and come. I love you and I welcome you.

Enjoying the Fruit of Your Labor

Entry #242

Fun days are ahead for you! Mark My words! I want to have fun with you! I want to show you the many wonders that I have created. It will cause you to well up with praises of thanksgiving! Oh, how I delight to show you My creation! I made it for you, you know. I want you to experience it and release its glorious wonders to others. It will come naturally!

You are truly entering a time of fullness, of tasting and seeing that I am surely good!! Although this time it is not just a taste, it is an overflowing! Past seasons were tastes, witnessing to you of the time you are now entering. Yes! The time has come, for you have made yourself ready with the capacity to hold all I want to give you! Thank you for your service; but more than anything, thank you for an unwavering heart that continues to love Me through every valley and mountain, every trial and victory! You have stood the test of time. I am so pleased, Beloved!

Come, enter in, and take a seat at My table. The banquet has been set for you, and now you are about to eat the fruits of your labor. What delight! What tasteful wonder! What joy wells up in My heart! I have waited for this day, Dear One. Yes, I have waited with eager anticipation! You have ravished My heart and I have granted you My Kingdom. Come! Eat your fill! For soon the music will start and we shall dance the night away in a glorious celebration!

My Delight Is a Light for All to See

Entry #243

I've created you and blessed you with a way to peak people's interest to search for Me. They are curious about what you're carrying. In fact, they've never quite seen someone like you. By watching your life, they will be willing to take the leap of faith to find Someone so real, so true, and beyond their wildest dreams! Once they take a drink of Me, they'll never be the same! You will offer Me as that drink to many, many people. It will be something they seek you for and you will give it at My leading and prompting. You will declare all the days of your life, "Taste and see that the Lord is good".

Stay in the courts of My praise all the days

of your life, for I am worthy and you will enjoy the fruit that comes bursting forth from the lips! I have adorned you and prized you as Mine! I take good care of those who belong to Me. You are always free to come into My heart. Make it your home and dwelling place forever. How blessed are those who live in My house, ever praising Me! You are truly My delight!

The Invitation to Enroll Further in My Training

Entry #244

Wisdom and Revelation are knocking at your door, ready to teach you the next things. Be open, listen, and learn for My Kingdom is always ready to teach those willing to learn. All I need from you is to be willing, expectant, and be ready to record what I'm about to teach you. Do you know that writing down My revelations is a sign to Me of your belief and faith? It puts your faith into action. Students always record what their teachers teach them, do they not? You are a good student of Mine. Those who seek shall find; and to those who ask, it shall be given.

Enrollment, too, is an act of faith. It is declaring what you want and what you want to advance in. Like I said, We (Papa, Son, and Holy Spirit), along with Wisdom and Revelation are more than willing to teach you. Remember My Word says that many are called, but few are chosen. Many are called to My classes in life, but few show up to enroll in them. Be one of those few that show up, for I have indeed called you. Be willing and pliable to receive the disciplines of your Teacher. They are meant to make you better and give you a sharp sense of direction and insight. I am teaching you discernment.

Let's discuss pain, for instance. Pain can often be for your gain if you process it right. Pain is a demise to those unwilling to learn from it. Pain is not always a bad thing. One endures it for the outcome it produces, hence "growing pains" or the growth of a muscle. Short-term pain can bring you compassion in areas you didn't have before. So, let's not always look at pain as a bad thing. Cash in on it and find the good! Don't waste these opportunities to learn, rather find something that will improve your well-being. This is the reason pain is allowed.

Now, not all pain is profitable and of Me. That is why I am in the process of teaching you discernment. Many bring unnecessary pain upon themselves. I will teach you how to decipher between the two.

Those who are trained by Me shall receive My mark and be recognized as one of My pupils. This is very important. You will be able to tell who the imposters are. Recognize them, but leave the judgments to Me. I am teaching you by My discipleship to simply do as I do. Follow Me and soon you will put out the call for others to follow you. In so doing My heritage and signature ways will be recognized by the many. There are distinct sounds and ways of living that I have ordained. All who follow Me and learn from My teaching will truly be a city set on a hill, a light for all men to see. So come, enroll yourself in My training, and I will teach you the ways of My Kingdom.

How to Have More of an Effortless Life and Healthy Friendships

Entry #245

It gives Me great pleasure to see My children enjoying the things I freely give them. Everything is free in heaven. There is no earning it. All you have to do is simply ask. It's only when you step outside your dependency on Me and reach for things on your own, that you find yourself removed from a place of provision. Isn't that what happened to Adam and Eve? Isn't that what becomes of a cut off branch on the ground removed from the vine? There is only death in man's efforts apart from Me. Life is found when engaged with Me. Efforts are not bad in themselves. It's all dependent upon who's leading them. Apart from Me, life will only yield by sweat and toil.

Effortless living is a new way of living. It is a joyful way of living. It's truly what I have intended. Just look back to the Garden and tell Me if that wasn't My heart and original plan. Yes, of course, it takes an effort to do anything. Truly it all comes down to the matters of the heart and who you choose to follow. Would you like to learn more about this effortless living, effortless in that it's not a burden, but a joy? Lean in and ask Me to teach you. It's going to take some change in your mindset, but the more you hang out with Me the more your ideas on life are going to change.

It's important who you hang around. Who you hang around influences the way you do and view life. Hanging out with Me will always profit you! I know you know that. All I'm doing is drawing your attention to and accounting for who is leading and influencing your life. Do your friends speak and think life or death? Whatever is in them will eventually transfer onto you. I placed this ability in mankind so that they would become imitators of Me. That is why you must guard yourself in the group you call your close friends. Assess if you want to become like them, for they will influence the decisions you make and the actions you take. Choose wisely. Set aside more time to be with Me. I am going to teach you about living life effortlessly. I am the healthiest friend you could ever have. Whatever is in Me will transfer to you and I will influence the decisions you make and the actions you take. Choose wisely.

We Want to be With You All the Time

Entry #246

Do you think the Temple model or church building is what We (Papa, Jesus, and Holy Spirit) intended? We never wanted to live in a temple or a building alone. Isn't that written all throughout My Scriptures? What can contain us? We never wanted mankind to just visit us once a week for a one to two-hour session on Sunday. We are grateful for all who come, but we want to be with mankind all the time! What parents would be able to stand seeing their children only once or twice a week for an hour or two? Wouldn't you miss out on so much?! I know many of you feel and understand what I'm talking about. We feel the same way about you! We love you immensely! You are a part of us! Why would we want to short change any time with you? We would rather dwell with you, live every day with you, and be there with you through thick and thin. We want to counsel you, guide you, and instruct you. We want to be there to encourage you and tell you how much We love and adore you! Don't you think that's a much better plan? Would you really think we didn't want to be that intimate and involved? How can love EVER be happy with separation? You tell Me! If We are love, how do you think We feel? Yes, We have feelings; who do you think created yours? Make us truly happy by inviting us into your everyday life. Here is where We'll stay and here is where we'll dwell. Our desire is to be one and with you. You are the habitation we delight in.

Are You Guessing at How to Live Your Life?

Entry #247

Have you entrusted your life into My hands? Let's just say you've taken off the pilot's hat and put it back on My head. This is an act of you trusting My flight plan over yours, a far better and safer route. I'll teach you the ropes as you learn from Me.

Many have chosen to do this backward. Many have made their own flight plan and have asked Me to bless it! There is a time where I will entrust you to make those decisions, but many have jumped straight out of the gate and into the plane all in the name of "Let's give this a try," "I'm doing this for God," or for the zeal of something new. They quit their day jobs, start-up churches, or leave for the mission field. None of this is wrong in itself. Their calling is real, but many have engaged in this through assumption and presumption, motivated and directed by their own ideas. They bypass talking to the owner, jump into the plane, roll out their own makeshift flight plan, and end up with a crash and burn on their hands. After this experience, they walk away from the plane with much regret, disappointment, confusion, and resentment for they had moved out in their own strength and power. They wanted to do something FOR Me, they proclaim. Assumption can be a dangerous thing. Assuming you can drive a car or plane without being properly trained will always lead to a deadly situation.

Let Me ask you this... If you received a plane for the very first time as a gift from the owner, would you jump in and guess at how to fly it? A humble man would ask the owner in detail about this gift. He would ask him to show and mentor him in how to fly it. He would also ask the owner what he should know about the plane; are there any special tricks to it, quirks, or unique ways of handling of it. He would ask what its maximum weight and capacity is. He would ask what the plane was specifically designed for, what its maximum speeds, altitudes, and flight distance is. These are just a few of the questions he would ask.

My gifts are freely given but few have asked Me how they work. Turn it back over to Me and let's begin this conversation with where you're at on the journey, who you are, what you have, and what I have in mind for you. It's safe to say that you can trust Me with your life. Now let's "fly" this "plane" together!

One of Your Greatest Weapons of Defense

Entry #248

Thanksgiving will build a backbone in you that no enemy can stand against. Thanksgiving makes you invisible to the enemy. Negativity opens doors to the enemy; being positive pushes the enemy back out and closes the door! Whichever way you choose to let it swing, you will give access to one or the other. Thanksgiving comes from within and releases outward. Negativity comes as an onslaught against you and weakens your defenses. Thanksgiving is a mighty weapon. If you want to cut off all the ropes of access to the enemy, then speak out your thanksgiving. It severs all the connections he had to shut you down.
 This is how you keep your heart and

house clean. I inhabit your praises and where I am the enemies will not come. They can't stand to look upon me.

You will want me filling your heart and house. My light confuses the enemies and blinds them, throwing them into a spinning chaos of their own demise. The more My light exudes from you, the greater the power you shall have. Welcome Me fully into every area of your life--your speech, your eyes, your ears, your mouth, your body and everything you set your hand to do. Consume Me and proclaim Me and you will penetrate your surroundings with unstoppable light and life! My desire is for us to be one and in sync with each other. I will do the work and be the changing force. All you need to do is welcome Me and praise Me. Your circumstances will change, your outlook will change, and your heart will change for the better.

Rest: The Ultimate Trademark

Entry #249

Rest is the greatest weapon on earth because it is a sign and statement of ultimate trust in Me. What was Jesus' stance, remember? He was asleep and at rest on the boat in the midst of the storm. Let Him truly be your example. Jesus came to bring the new way of the Kingdom. Remember he said many times, "I am the way! So come, follow Me". (Matt 11:28)

I want your life to be a contrast from the way most people live on this earth. How can there be light and salt without a contrast? People should see and taste the difference in you and notice the difference in the peace that encompasses you. Remember, like I've always said, the more time you spend with Me, the more you'll look like Me, talk like Me, smell like Me, and feel like Me. It's that simple. People become like who they hang around. If you hang out with REST, My Son, the Prince of Peace, you'll become peace. He's already in you; it's just a matter of engaging in a continual relationship with Him.

I Will Take You through the Storm

Entry #250

I am fully aware of everything that is going on in your life right now. Throw your anchor onto Me. I am the sure foundation that will see you through! Rest, rest, rest in the boat. It's time to take shelter under My wings. Lean into Me and watch the storms pass. Know that My arms are tightly wrapped around you. You won't miss My leading, you won't miss My prompting. You can trust Me to guide you right on through. Sink your heart into Mine and let Me be your abode. Take a sigh of relief for relief is surely on its way. Breathe deep, breathe slow, and know that everything's OK. All My purposes work together and in this way, good shall abound. You can trust Me with your journey. Give Me a little more credit than you have. Believe that I care more than you thought. Trust that I love you deeper than you ever knew, for all this is so very true. One day you'll know the why behind it all. Start believing now and soon you'll see it show. Declare that I am your safe place!

Watch Me sail you through this difficulty. The more you lean on Me the stronger you will be. I am building confidence in you; a sure, rock-solid foundation. I not only want you to know about Me, but I want you to experience Me coming through for you time and time again. I am worth trusting and I am worth waiting for. Sing and shout your praise! Thankfulness draws My breath like a powerful wind, blowing and filling your sails to succeed. More than a team effort, this is really a love response, a trust response, a believing that all things work together for good response. I've got you, Sweet One, I've got you!

Surrender in Action

Entry #251

"Lord, how do I live a life of surrender with action attached?" "Follow Me, your good shepherd, wherever I lead you. Stay close enough to hear me. If you can't quite hear Me yet, then come even closer; close enough to feel My leading and prompting, to hear My gentle whisper. Lovers whisper, you know..."

Surrender seems foolish to mankind. You live in a culture and society that views surrender as giving up! I view it as giving up, too; but not in the way man looks at it, for you could not possibly give something up to Me. Ego will always <u>E</u>dge Me (<u>G</u>od) <u>O</u>ut. When you surrender or "give up", you acknowledge that your leadership over your life is not suitable, so you hand the reins back to Me. Now that is a very wise decision. But guess what? We're still in the same cart together. You've just chosen to allow wisdom to take the reins.

Surrender with action means you're following instead of leading and stepping out on your own. You are acknowledging Me as your shepherd and protector. You can leave whenever you want. I am not a controlling Father. I've given you a free will, but love will choose to trust and stay. Love is what I'm after. A surrendered heart that is saying, "I surrender to love."

A prideful heart breaks rank. Maybe what you're really asking is, "Lord, how can I *achieve* something with a surrendered heart?" Watch out for the subtleties of independence and significance. Test your heart, My dear one. If you are frustrated and looking for a sense of value apart from Me, it will lead you straight into an independent spirit. Remember the story of the prodigal son. Guard yourself and reassess where the disconnection is. There are two tracks of action, one leads to following your shepherd and the other to following your pride. Test your heart and see what's motivating it.

Surrendering with action is a "preferring" love language; a yoking together in partnership, learning to walk in sync and rhythm with each other. I've placed good desires within you. Let's walk together and discuss them. Share with Me your ideas; this is a partnership of two lovers creating. When I say follow Me, I'm not referring to a subjection to dominance, for again you're free to go anytime you like. Love cannot be love without someone to love, and love is expressed by action and responses. Surrendering with action is simply preferring and responding in a covenant of love.

The I.D. Check on Provision

Entry #252

Yes, Provision. Many of My people, including you, have been crying out for Me to teach them about provision. It's really simple. What's difficult for most is the effort of staying consistent. The first thing you're going to have to do is chuck an orphan mentality and accept your true inheritance. You cannot have an orphan soul and expect wealth to be attracted to you. A generous heart attracts wealth. Orphans can be self-centered and selfish, focused only on their increase and importance. They've lived a life of survival and self-sufficiency. So in order for you to have wealth if you've struggled in this area, you must first accept and take on your new identity in Christ.

You have a new name and all kinds of

wealth that come with it! But if you haven't changed your old name and the old one is still showing on your new nature

"license," you won't be given access as easily. There must be a transition for a transfer to take place. Once you've changed your identity, others will witness it and give you the access that comes with that name. Heaven will also respond. I am not a poor God, but I am a just God and a king of precepts and order. Your "bank account," "license," and "passport" must all be aligned to My Kingdom for access. A false identity will never do. Wealth is not about acquiring. It is about identity, permission, alignment, and acknowledgment. Those who believe they are who I say they are and act accordingly shall inherit the wealth allotted to them.

It's all about the name on the I.D. I have given My children access. It is up to them to exchange their old identification for the new. The more you walk in this, the more doors will open to you and prosperity will be drawn to you. Engage in who you are and what I've given you. Sow and invest in your new identity and more will be added to you.

No Need to Apologize

Entry #253

There's no need to apologize. You are simply going through the process. I want you to let go of the wondering and just keep declaring that you trust Me! I am patient with you, now be patient with yourself. Do you know you'll get a better response from yourself if you're more patient with yourself? Grace, grace, grace, Sweet One! If you allow yourself some grace, you'll not only give it to yourself, but you'll give it to others. You'll find yourself enjoying life more this way. I am giving you permission to do this. There's no catch. You're simply responding to yourself and others through heaven's culture and not through this world's. Isn't that what you crave? And I guarantee it's what others crave as well. No more apologizing. I've already forgiven you years ago! Satisfy My heart by receiving My forgiveness.

I know you live caught between two worlds, My Kingdom and the world's dictates. It's like mixed signals are crossing your path all the time. But as with any new thing, it takes time to adjust, to recognize the counterfeits and to embrace the true. Think about it like learning a new language; one cannot learn Japanese overnight. I want you to allow grace to work in your life in the same way. All I desire from you is a willing heart. I'm not focused on any mistakes. I'm always only looking at your heart and your continual willingness to follow Me.

Grace is like an energy pill; the more you receive it the more you'll thrive. It's meant to keep you close to Me. Sin will always cause you to distance yourself. Grace is like a magnet. When you receive it, it automatically draws you back to Me! The Good News is forgiveness and a better way of living. Whatever you receive from Me you'll be able to easily give to others. Here's the trick to receiving--turn your eyes from looking at yourself and look at

Me. Change your hands from covering yourself; open them up and receive My covering, love, forgiveness, and life. It's already paid for.

Why Is Stillness a Challenge?

Entry #254

Stillness...why is it so hard for My people? Have you ever stopped and asked yourself why you're so busy? What is all this busyness for? How much of it is driven by love, how much of it is driven by fear, and how much of it is driven by obligation? My people have lost touch with their hearts. If fear is your motivation, then how can you have peace? What are you afraid of? Are you afraid you'll discover the truth when you still yourself? What do you think the truth is? What if what you believe the truth is, is not the truth? What if in stillness you'll find the answers you're longing for, the answers that you've been trying to find in your busyness?

Busyness can be the long way around, believe it or not. If you'll take some time to sit with Me, I'll lead you to a better way than the "short cuts" as you may call them. Don't you think I already know what you need? Wouldn't you rather ask someone with wisdom than try to figure it out yourself? That's just a waste of energy. I'm your inside scoop, your hidden resources. I'm the one that can give you the cutting edge and put you above the rest. And you know what's even better? It can all be done from a state of rest.

You have a direct line with Me, like the red phone to the white house, but even better! You have a relationship with Me. I have the answers and the wisdom and in that wisdom, I will show you a far better way. All that's required is that you still yourself; still your heart. Come unto Me, into My garden, into a peaceful place and reconnect with Me. It's what your heart wants, but your mind has been convincing you that you don't have time. Is that really true or just an excuse of misplaced priorities? Make the time and you'll make out far better.

I want you to be an example and a light to the world. They are all looking for a better way. If you resemble their cookie cutter system, you'll only lead them in fruitless circles of what they already have. Give them what they don't have. Show them what they're missing; a truly blissful, directed, restful life in Me that far exceeds the crowds. Apart from Me you can do nothing, but with Me all things are possible. I've created you to have life and that more abundantly. Make a transaction today and trade what you've been doing for the option I'm presenting you. You won't regret it. It will be to your credit! Stillness is the key to unlocking your destiny. All you need to know is found in Me.

What's My Responsibility?

Entry #255

Often times you ask Me, "What's my responsibility"? I would answer you with this... Your responsibility is to trust Me. That is your response and your ability tied together. Together they form response-ability. You have the ability to trust Me and I want that to be your response. So, are you in?

Oftentimes people take on responsibility as a form of duty. Oftentimes they steer away from its true root meaning. Go look it up. My people have focused so much on the duty part that they've forgotten the heart of the word, which is "response." What is your response going to be; one of faith or one of fear? Your ability will either align you with one or the other. Actions follow thoughts, thought responses. So, that leads to an even deeper question. What are your thoughts right now and how are you processing them and choosing to respond to them? What actions would you like to follow through with? My desire is that your response would always be one of faith and trust. You'll reap a good result if you choose those.

There is a role to play in responsibility, a role of faith or a role of fear. One takes you higher and one takes you lower. In the Garden of Eden, Adam and Eve were given the ability to choose, and it was their response that led to their final outcome. Your responsibility is not so much the act that follows as it is the choice to believe. What I am asking is for you to simply respond by belief. That is your responsibility, not mine. My responsibility is to respond to your faith by My ability to answer the desire of your heart. See how that works? It's not complicated like man likes to make it. It's truly a dance or an exchange, a form of communication. Communicate to Me by your response of faith. The rest is sure to fall in line accordingly.

Recommendations from Your Heart Doctor

Entry #256

Out of the heart, the mouth speaks. So, what have you been saying? It's time to take a closer examination. Not to shame yourself. No, by all means no! But to simply take an assessment of what you believe. What you believe reveals what you are truly ingesting and it is now coming out of your pores, one of those being your mouth. Listen to your words. Listen to your self-talk and what you say about others and to others. Listen to what you say about life, your situation, and your relationships. What comes out of your mouth is coming out of your heart. Pay attention to your symptoms...

I am the Great Physician and it's time you

schedule an appointment with Me. Come into My "office." I am going to prescribe to you a miracle cure: Input = output. If you take this prescription, you're going to see a change in your well-being and your symptoms will disappear.

Doing this will heal your loneliness of heart. Your words have brought about this symptom. I'd like to offer you the value and sense of belonging you've been looking for. It will change your life forever, but you must be persistent in following My recommendations. What's in this prescription? Life and that more abundantly, the way of life Christ offers! He's already taken care of all the cost for you. In fact, if you live by this way of life, you'll receive a life of "second chances." Believe it or not, you'll walk out of here with a whole new identity and outlook on life! Your friends won't recognize you! They are going to ask you what's changed. Your reply could simply be, "Just following the doctor's orders..."

Whether this is your first time seeing Me or you are here for a check-up, I am here to guide you in the path of healing for what your symptoms have been alerting you. So, where does it all start? It starts with the heart, and that is why you are here in My "office" right now having this conversation with me. Let Me take a look at your heart. Open it up and turn it towards Me. Follow My recommendations and you'll live the fulfilled life I've planned for you; full of happiness, meaning, and love. You'll be walking in your destiny...straight into eternity and health.

How Does Faith Come?

Entry #257

How does faith come? My people keep begging Me for more faith, but I have already told them that faith comes by hearing... and hearing My Word. That's it. There is no other way. You cannot add more to faith. It is simply agreeing with what I've already spoken to you. There are no levels to faith. The only thing that is changing and increasing is your willingness to believe Me. That is where the expansion is. You can pray all you want, but this is a matter of the will. It's so simple you can miss it. It's not a matter of attaining; it's a matter of choosing to agree and believe versus choosing to disagree and disbelieve.
If you want to pray for anything, pray for more courage to believe Me and My words. Faith is like an on and off light switch. If you believe the light bulb in the

room will do what it's meant to do, then you'll turn that light switch on! You'll do it even without the evidence of light appearing first. It's a "switch" of the will. It's so simple My people miss it all the time. You either choose to believe or you don't. The reason most people don't believe is that they have not allowed it to enter their hearts. They've heard it in form but have not allowed it to become a part of them. Sometimes this can be like a little child resisting swallowing his food and then spitting it out. My people spit out My food with their reason and logic. Please give it more time. Chew on it and allow it to do what it's supposed to do; nourish you and help you grow into who you were created to be. Faith is a choice, not a feeling. Do you need to feel to turn on a light switch? Well, doesn't that say it all? You choose to flip the switch and the light turns on. Think of faith this way and you'll watch all that you believe for come to life! Faith is a choice. Turn on the Light!

The end

Papa's Living Room Vol. 2

For more info about the author, and more in depth details about The Papa's Living Room please read Papa's Living Room Vol. 1. You can purchase a copy on Amazon or by going to our site:

www.thrivingculture.org

NOTES

NOTES

NOTES

Made in the USA
Columbia, SC
20 October 2017